My Favourite Person

Someone Special To Me
Edited by Connie Hunt

First published in Great Britain in 2009 by:

Young Writers
Remus House
Coltsfoot Drive
Peterborough
PE2 9JX
Telephone: 01733 890066
Website: www.youngwriters.co.uk

All Rights Reserved
Book Design by Spencer Hart & Tim Christian
© Copyright Contributors 2009
SB ISBN 978-1-84924-698-9

Foreword

Our 'My Favourite Person 2009' poetry competition attracted young aspiring poets to show their admiration for those who have made an impact in their life. What better way to let those closest know how much they are appreciated.

We are delighted to present 'Someone Special To Me'. After reading through the hundreds of entries it is clear the amount of enthusiasm and love that went into writing these poems, therefore we hope you'll agree they are an inspiring and heart-warming read.

Young Writers was established in 1991 to promote poetry and creative writing to schoolchildren and encourage them to read, write and enjoy it. Here at Young Writers we are sure you'll agree that this special edition achieves our aim and celebrates today's wealth of young writing talent. We hope you enjoy 'Someone Special To Me' for many years to come.

Contents

Ahmed Aboukoura (13) 1
Shormee Aziz (14) 2
Bethany Warlow (11) 3
Melissa O'Neill (13) 4
Lucy Jones (12) 5
Chantelle McSharry (15) 6
Sinead Marlow (13) 7
Claudia Watson (11) 8
Ellis Watkinson (13) 9
Antonia Roberts (15) 10
Courteney Barker (10) 10
Ryan McAteer (11) 11
Aimee Hunter (10) 11
Chelsea Clancy (13) 12
Daniel Holliday (15) 13
Molly Howarth (9) 14
Alanah Kiernan (6) 14
Eleanor Martin (9) 15
Joseph McKenna (8) 15
Zoe McConkey (12) 16
Niamh Porter (9) 16
Cecilia Micklethwaite (12) 17
Shannon Wigley (8) 17
Megan Rose Hopper (10) 18
Dionne Burgin (9) 18
Christiana Oladokun 19
Emma Harrison (11) 19
Niccole Matthews (15) 20
Jessica Broughton (9) 20
Tiahna Joshi (10) 21
Kate Brown (12) 21
Alexia McGuinness (11) 22
Roheen Nawaz (11) 22
Jude Hunt (11) 23
Hannah Smith (12) 23
Amy Nicole Mann (11) 24
Josh Miles (11) 24
Issac Cross-Costello (11) 25
Maddison Rourke (8) 25
Emma Dunbar (11) 26
Emily Rose Tweedale (12) 26

Adaeze Ebodili (11) 27
Jessica Ellis 27
Sam Davidson-Pennington (11) 28
Susie Concannon (11) 28
Rebecca Emma Guy (10) 29
Chloe Collins (11) 29
Alice Mason (10) 30
Kate Appleton (11) 30
Grace Richards (10) 31
Clara Kevin (11) 31
Naomi Wrigley (10) 32
Emma Kennedy (10) 32
Jemma McIvor (6) 33
Sophia Hume (10) 33
Erin Thompson (10) 34
Crystal Daniels (6) 34
Christopher Bentley (10) 35
Eryn Lamble (10) 35
Lauren McComb (10) 36
Jasmine Cargan (10) 36
Hannah Boniface (12) 37
Charlotte Clews (10) 37
Majidah Begum (9) 38
Charlie Rogers-Smith (11) 38
Imogen Daisy Clay (10) 39
Thomas Peters 39
Jessica Peers (13) 40
Amina Miah (11) 40
Katie Quirk (9) 41
Jenny Law (7) 41
Georgia Clark (10) 42
Louise Firth (11) 42
Jack Elliot Culver (10) 43
Ryan Howitt (11) 43
Maya Sharda 44
Ellie Farmer (12) 44
Katie Clarke (13) 45
Matilda Burnie (8) 45
Zoë Elena Beckett (11) 46
Grace Bird (10) 46
Lauren Fiddes (10) 47

Casey Haslam (10)	47
Leah Lafferty (10)	48
Alice Payne (10)	48
Emily Wilson (10)	49
Lauren Gibson (13)	49
Georgie McKenzie Smith (11)	50
Venus MacKenzie (10)	50
Hannah Rusling (12)	51
Bethanie Mortenson (8)	51
Luke McCarron (10)	52
Harry Thewlis (10)	52
Ryan McMahon (11)	53
Aimee May Walker (13)	53
Tasharna Patrick (12)	54
Carla McKeagney (9)	54
Olivia Mailey (11)	55
Alice Talbot (11)	55
Emily Tullett (10)	56
Jennifer Irwin (11)	56
Courtney Green (11)	57
Ami Paterson (10)	57
Blair Gibson (11)	58
Shannon Louise Smith (12)	58
Austen Lowe (12)	59
Jasmine Azaei (11)	59
Callum O'Shaugnessy (9)	60
Indira Fernando (11)	60
Melissa Morton (10)	61
Mabel Osejindu (15)	61
Esme Challis (10)	62
Dominic Leake (10)	62
Benjamin Harris (11)	63
Josephine Gibbs (8)	63
Madeline Charlemagne (11)	64
Caitlin Devenney (10)	64
Anas Aboukoure (9)	65
Megan Paul (15)	65
Leanne Cooper (10)	66
Francesca Spolverino (10)	66
Lynne Davidson (11)	67
Jake Lafferty (9)	67
Amy Langston (13)	68
Alex Gordon (10)	68
Eunice Koroma (7)	69
Becky Rose Knowles (10)	69
Matthew Buckby (8)	70
Katie Fairhurst (11)	70
Hannah Pomfret (11)	71
Sameerah Shaikh (11)	71
Ana Young (11)	72
Alice Allen (14)	72
Lucy Turpin (11)	73
Sarmad Khan (8)	73
Charlotte Gosling (14)	74
Emmie Clark (11)	74
Molly Ellis (9)	75
Caitlin Penrice (11)	75
Glenn Doncaster (10)	76
Victoria Deery (11)	76
Arabella Dolores Petts (10)	77
Sally Pierse (10	77
Abbie Williams (10)	78
Tyla Thomas (11)	78
Tiegan Stanford (11)	79
Jack McElroy (10)	79
Shannon Thwaite (11)	80
Leah Scott (11)	80
Hannah Giddens (11)	81
Elizabeth Richards (11)	81
Lara Jobling (10)	82
Amelia Robins (9)	82
Veerinder Kaur Gill (9)	83
Finlay Cardno (10)	83
Melissa Ward (10)	84
Tiffany-Jayne Bull (13)	84
Chloe Runkee (13)	85
Mohammad Abdullah (13)	85
Nell McCall (6)	86
Alice Parkes (8)	86
Emilie Riley (14)	87
Kerri Lorraine (10)	87
Merran Paxton (11)	88
Victoria Jenkins (8)	88
Alisha Allman (13)	89
Isabelle Marie Rayworth (10)	89
Bethany McTrustery (14)	90
Emma Calvey (14)	90
Jordan Brown (11)	91
Ibara Razaq (12)	91
Rheanna Egleton (10)	92

Ashton Broxholme (6)	92
Gemma Williams (11)	93
Olivia Jackson (10)	93
Cara Marenghi (10)	94
Iona Newman (10)	94
Declan Whatmough (9)	95
Klaudia Robinson (10)	95
Kyle Dunnel (11)	96
Chloe McDonald (10)	96
Sydney Horne (12)	97
Charlotte Marsh (11)	97
Tanjima Akhtar (11)	97
Zainab Sattar (13)	98
Aqsa Mahmud (11)	98
Jamie-Lee Jaeger (10)	98
Jack Stiles (11)	99
April Lukanu (11)	99
Lauryn Dickinson (7)	99
Samantha Hardman (10)	100
Danielle Davies (9)	100
Emma Ferguson (11)	100
Jordan Burnett (8)	101
Hazera Begum (9)	101
Holly O'Connor (10)	101
Abigail Munro (9)	102
Georgia Thornton (8)	102
Asha Wilkinson (10)	102
Mohammad Ibara Ali Razaq (12)	103
Amirah Sattar (17)	103
Nicole Thorneycroft (13)	103
Declan Parker (11)	104
Courtney Legan (11)	104
Shannon Miller (10)	104
Jordyn Rosser (11)	105
Lubabah Khan (11)	105
Melissa Rodda (10)	105
Emma Caro (9)	106
Siril Sunny (10)	106
Daniela Windram (11)	106
Sophie Newton (8)	107
Heather Robertson (10)	107
Jason Poom (9)	107
Elly Jackson (11)	108
Ella Hull (8)	108
Luke Richardson (6)	108
Katherine Gill (11)	109
Charlotte Wade (11)	109
Natasha Chappell (11)	109
Frankie Tulley (11)	110
Chloe Anne Hunter (11)	110
Emily Allen (11)	110
Nikaela Cruikshank (11)	111
Daniel Morton (11)	111
Eilidh-Jane Murphy (10)	111
Dylan Foster (10)	112
Falak Khan (7)	112
Lauren Richardson (12)	112
Shannon Hill (10)	113
Elizabeth Lovejoy (12)	113
Tianna Costelow (11)	113
Neal McCulloch (9)	114
Hannah Chambers (11)	114
Sabia Shafiq (10)	114
Yasmin Martin (9)	115
Dillon Marsden (11)	115
Sam Knapman (11)	115
Jessica Milner (9)	116
Phoebe Corser (15)	116
Catarina Alves (8)	116
Rhiannon Burrows (12)	117
Abdul Baasit Mahmood (11)	117
Eleanor Gabriel (10)	117
Lauren Siely (9)	118
Adam Wilkinson (11)	118
Aimee Ford (11	118
Alexander Jessiman (11)	119
David Triano (10)	119
Claudia Law (10)	119
Gemma Wells (12)	120
Jodi Morgan (11)	120
Thomas Oliver (10)	120
Kimberley Breingan (11)	121
Shannon Turney (10)	121
Tajalla Rasool (12)	121
Brandon Parkin (10)	122
Amy Louise Crain (11)	122
Megan Jarvis (10)	122
Jamie Lee Hopps (10)	123
Arooj Khan (10)	123
Matthew Whelan (6)	123

Katelyn Grant (11).................................124
Kayleigh Wickenden (10).....................124
Beth Cushnie (9)....................................124
Abbie Kiernan (8) 125
Arron Finnis (9).....................................125
Tahlia Walker (11) 125
Sam Patrick (10)....................................126

The Poems

My Favourite Person - Someone Special To Me

Obama

Radiating perpetual streams of glory.
Rearing towards Heaven aloft a great golden podium.
Before him, seas of men cry.
An egg in what he is to become.

Obama! We jeer, buffeted by thousands of men.
He stands, gleaming like a star.
Charged with colossal ambition.
He can reach so far.

Obama, the glimmer of hope in these troublesome feuds.
Exquisite in every way.
We can only claw at his feet.
As he enters the fray.

Obama, my solitary idol.
He vaults effortlessly over barriers.
Glides easily over rivers.
Unable to deter.

Obama, saviour of the world.
An angel from the skies.
My hero, my solitary hero.
The one whom I idolise.

Obama, a rose in a festoon of weeds.
A golden coin in a mountain of silver.
Unique, different, superb . . .
To infer.

It is not his power that is great.
His kindness glows and twinkles.
In the nebulous sky.
Propels.

Can he save us . . . ?
Yes he can!

Ahmed Aboukoura (13)

A True Legend

Michael Jackson, who? Yeah he's the king,
The reason for good music, it revolved around him,
The giving, the loving, he was the true king
You see what I'm tryin' to say is just bow to a legend,
For a second let your thoughts be on a passing legend,
I appreciate him, I appreciate them,
Who are they?
The Jackson family for always giving forever till no end.

And when my days were cold and so bitter,
I'd play MJ's music, tracks like 'Thriller',
And listen to his sad words from 'You Are Not Alone',
And bury them in my mind, for now, my hero is gone,
And I'd dance to 'Billie Jean', and try out the famous moonwalk,
Letting the music sink in, and my tears they'd never stop,
And although I was born in '95, I'd skim through music back from '75,
And watch him dance in the Jackson 5,
Singing, 'I'll Be There', I loved watching him live.

He made the world dance, he made us all sing,
Joining God's great big family with tracks like,
'Heal the World', making us believe,
That it doesn't matter if you're black,
No it doesn't matter if you're white,
What matters is what is inside
So I'm singing this freestyle,

MJ, you were the one that showed me,
That I can be who I wanna be,
And every day when I got bullied,
And every day when I was worried,
I turned to your music
Dancing and singing, no one could quite sing like you did,
What a loss now that you're gone,
My tears won't stop and I feel alone,
But your legacy will live on,
And you'll live in our hearts,

The king that tried to better us,
As no one can thrill us like MJ dancing the thriller,
Or quite do the moonwalk like he did in 'Billie Jean',
Or give as much to charity like the 300 million he donated,

We all know you tried to change the world and make it a better place,
Now I look up in the sky and hope that you're in a better place,
So it's bow to him, for losing him was such grief,
The king of pop, the loving and giving, the legend that had lived.

Shormee Aziz (14)

My Mum

I love my mum
She is the best,
Although I put her to the test,
She has blonde hair,
Which is *never* a mess,
But this I say with some duress,
Make her cross, she's a lioness.

I love my mum,
She likes to cook,
And make me things from a large cook book,
I gobble it all up and leave no trace,
Except the bits I leave on my face!

I love my mum
She is there for me,
Whether I cut myself,
Or I'm stung by a bee,
She cleans the wounds,
Puts a plaster on,
Then *hey presto the pain is gone!*

I love my mum
She is very neat,
She loves to dance to a funky beat,
She spins around the living room floor,
Through the kitchen and out the back *door!*

Bethany Warlow (11)

My Favourite Person

My favourite person?
Who could that be?
A couple of clues will tell you
Who this might be.

He was born in America in 1929
He was born in Tennessee
He was a Baptist
Who could this be?

Could it be a pope
Or maybe a Baptist priest
Who could this mystery person be?
Maybe someone who served at a feast?

He was influenced by Rosa Parks
Another fighter
He turned people's lives around
And made them brighter.

He died a hero to everyone
Across the world and back
This might be a better clue
He was a dark-skinned black.

This mystery is nearly unravelled
So can you guess who it is
This person was very calm
And didn't get in a tizzy.

Now it's the end of the poem
Another quick clue, is that they could sing
Any guesses?
Yes, it was Martin Luther King.

Yes!
Martin Luther King is my favourite person for his bravery.

Melissa O'Neill (13)

My Little Cat Jessie

Already five years old when I was born,
Twin kittens, not at all like each other.
How could they share the same planet
Let alone the same mother?
Born striped like tigers, with green eyes so bright,
Snowy-white tummies and paws wintry-white.
But the likeness there ended. Polly plump and cuddly,
Liked to be stroked and sit on your knee.
Lay in the sunshine, never once climbed a tree.
But Jessie, so slim, so proud and so sleek,
Her character was flawed, had a bold, wicked streak.
Try to stroke her, she'd turn with a snarl and a hiss,
Her claws flashing, she'd strike, and seldom she'd miss.
Fierce, independent, never shied from a fight,
A great hunter, catching birds in mid-flight.
Frogs and mice, any creatures she'd slay,
Then drop them back home in a messy display.

Then four years ago, Polly got ill and she died.
My sister and I clung together and cried
And Jessie who hated her when she was alive
Searched the house relentlessly.
Oh Polly where did you hide?

I am now twelve, she's five years older than me,
A little old cat, quite pathetic to see.
Once a loner, seeks company wherever we be,
At night she now always sleeps on my bed,
And even lets me stroke her sweet head.
No longer can jump onto her favourite chair,
So gently I lift her and place her there
And when she dies I know I shall mourn,
My constant companion since the day I was born,
My little cat, Jessie.

Lucy Jones (12)

Friends Forever

Friends forever is how it's going to be, Lisa is her name.
You together along with me,
Stuck together as if with glue,
I could not be separated from you,
You turned around a really sad day,
Making it funny in every way.
As we grew up it stayed the same,
The parting time never came,
Many people thought it should,
But we knew it never would,
Because together we will stay,
Nothing can ever drive us away,
Together forever?
Apart never!
Lisa is my hero, she is like a drug,
I can't get enough of her friendship,
I'm addicted.
Lisa is like money,
I must have more and more of it.
Lisa is very strong,
And never wrong.
Doesn't tell lies, and uses her brain wise.
Therefore my best friend Lisa is my hero
And I gladly say she is my hero,
As she is there for me every single day.
She is my favourite person 'cause she isn't just my best friend,
She's like a sister, part of the family
And best of all she is my best friend
And I couldn't ask for a better person.
I love her very, very much!

Chantelle McSharry (15)

Someone I Admire

When anyone says that they admire someone, the one person that spring to mind is my granny, Annie Marlow. While most people pick their parents, I choose my granny because she has been through a lot, seen a lot and done a lot.

She was born and raised in a small house in Aughdulla Dromore.
At the age of five she began to attend the Drumlish primary school.
After leaving school she became a housewife.

She then married my grandad, James Marlow and so her name changed from Annie Harper to Annie Marlow. She then moved to a small house outside of Fintona. She had seven children but unfortunately the eldest girl, Patricia was a stillbirth. Then her husband unfortunately was diagnosed with a mental illness and died. She remained at her home.

All of her children were married off, except for her second youngest, Christy, who remained with his mother.

Then my cousin Jolene Marlow, aged 17, died in the Omagh bombing.

Around five years after the death of my cousin, another tragedy struck, which shook us all, Vinnie, the youngest of the family was found dead. He too had been diagnosed with a mental illness.
After many years the family decided she would stay with her daughter Margaret who had a house outside Seskinore. This is where she remains. She is now aged 87.

She has grey curly hair which is always brushed back from her face. The wrinkles sit on her face like hills. Her smile is like a row of white pearls. Her eyes tell the story of her life, the ups and downs.

Even today, she sits with a smile across her face, laughing at jokes and telling her own. I admire her because she has shown me, no matter what happens, to come out smiling and remember, there's always tomorrow.

Sinead Marlow (13)

My Little Sister

My little sister is so bad,
Yesterday she bit my dad,
The day before she pulled my hair,
And toddled off without a care,
Three days ago our cat bit her,
But that's because she pulled his fur,
She often loses my homework,
And when I look I'll see her smirk!
Her pictures she rips,
And paint pots she tips,
Then casually out of the room she skips!
She plays with her food,
When she's in a bad mood,
Even if it's already been chewed!
But when she's nice she really is sweet,
And the monkey within her is very discreet,
She charms with her smile,
To escape from exile,
She makes me laugh,
When we're sharing a bath,
And turns me to happy and overjoyed,
When before I was feeling sad or annoyed!
Nice pictures she draws,
She holds open doors,
And helps Mum to mop all the washable floors!
She tidies her things, and her glittering wings,
And tries not to fiddle with Mum's precious rings!
She can be a pest, but may I suggest,
That my little sister is just the best!

Claudia Watson (11)

My Grandad

As I look up into his smiling face,
I see an angel none can replace.
With his beautiful eyes and dazzling smile,
He makes every day of our lives worthwhile.
I went to see him the other day,
He smiled at me in his dazzling way.
He told me he loved me and gave me a kiss,
This is one of the things I really shall miss.
He loves to watch cricket and rugby on telly,
Always keeps his hands folded neatly on his belly.
Wearing a hat and driving a red car,
He's the best grandad in the whole world by far.
My grandad pretends that he has long hair,
He likes to play games with us and boy, does he care!
We sometimes go over to sleep there at night,
In the dark, his eyes are always so bright.
He loves my nan's cooking and eats every bit,
And when he has finished he wants more of it!
He never moans or shouts at me,
He always laughs going *hee hee hee*.
Any pain, my granddad will cure,
Because his love is amazingly pure.
My grandad smells of newly-bought soap,
His heart is filled with confidence and hope.
My grandad, he is one of the best,
But once he's been my hero, he always needs a rest!
I give him a hug and kiss him goodnight,
And smile at the stars that are shining so bright.

Ellis Watkinson (13)

He's A Hero To Me

The very first time that I saw his face,
He was travelling about time and in space,
A military coat, worn on his back,
The stunning con man called Captain Jack.
He charms everyone with his dazzling grin,
With his eyes so bright and his perfect skin.
Actor John Barrowman stole my heart,
I was mesmerized with him from the start.
Started off being a small confession,
Now people say it is an obsession.
I say it is not but they do not know,
That John Barrowman, is my hero.
There's one thing I love, much more than his looks,
No it's not his films or even his books.
It's his personality, I adore,
To me perfection, I can't find a flaw.
He's got power to make me laugh or cry,
This John Barrowman is a wonderful guy.
There's much more to him than your eyes will see
On screen and off, he's a hero to me.
Always makes me smile when I hear his voice,
And seeing his face, I grin without choice.
I'm not embarrassed to say or to tell,
He's got me enchanted under his spell.
For this man is brilliant and he's a star,
To all future idols he's raised the bar.
I can't see him replaced anytime near,
For this man, I love him so very dear.

Antonia Roberts (15)

My Grandad

Grandad you help me when I'm struggling
And when I'm feeling down.
I love having you to turn my frown upside down.

Courteney Barker (10)

My Little Friend

My cat Yasmine, I got her when she was seven weeks old.
Now she is twenty-four weeks old,
And still doesn't do what she is told.
She can jump pretty high!
Sometimes more than I.

When she first came home she was a bit shy.
When you tell her off she will cry.
My cat Yasmine is so cute,
But sometimes you wish you could put her on mute.

Her eyes change colour from yellow to green,
But she still can be mean.
Very soon she learned to climb,
She has also done her own little crimes.

Yasmine has a mother and three brothers,
I wouldn't swap her for another.
One time they had a little fight,
It wasn't a pretty sight.

Yasmine is four different colours, orange, black, brown and white
And she is very light.
She plays football with her little ball
And she dives and falls.

My little cat, I love her so much.
But her toys she won't let you touch.
Everything I do she attends.
That's all about my little friend.

Ryan McAteer (11)

My Little Brother

My little brother is cute and sweet
And he likes a lot to eat.
He is fun. He likes playing with his balloons.
He is helpful and that is my little brother!

Aimee Hunter (10)

Time flies!

Time flies when you're having fun,
In the garden in the sun,
On the swings at the park,
In the sea playing sharks.
Time flies when you're having fun,
Eating chocolate, burgers and buns,
Playing the Xbox and PS3
On your laptop and Wii.
Time flies when you're having fun,
Sitting on the sofa or chasing the one,
Snuggling up and climbing trees,
Catching frogs and birds and bees!
Time flies when you're having fun,
Playing games with dad and mum,
Painting pictures and getting wet
Catching fish in the net.
Time flies when you're having fun,
Playing cops with a toy gun,
Jumping around on a hype,
With you're friends on a bike.
Time flies when you're having fun,
Time flies when you're having fun,
Time flies when you're having fun,
So remember when they are alone,
We can still have lots of fun
Remembering all the favourite things
At night-time in you're dreams.

Chelsea Clancy (13)

My Mother

Full of fun with a dashing smile,
To help me she'd even run a mile.
With chestnut brown hair and eyes,
She makes the sun shine in the skies.

My favourite person has to be,
My mother who is special to me.

She is my taxi and my chef,
She'll be here from birth to death.
A friendly shoulder to stop the pain,
She does everything for me without gain.

My favourite person has to be,
My mother who is special to me.

When the problems start she appears,
Wiping my eyes free from tears.
Throughout the years with no pay,
Working hard until she's grey.

My favourite person has to be,
My mother who is special to me.

She buys my clothes and all my food,
But I don't thank her, not that I'm rude.
Guiding and advising in all I do,
Showing that her love is true.

My favourite person has to be,
My mother who is special to me.

Daniel Holliday (15)

Our Super Nana

Maker of mask, costume and clothes,
Each of us have one, all specially wove.
She stitches on buttons, Velcro too,
They look like she bought them, completely brand new.

She's our super nana and we think she's cool.
She's our super nana, a fabulous jewel.

Well she's a fantastic chef, with scrumptious food,
I think her secret's her kind-hearted mood.
We wish for the Thursdays to come even quicker,
Yummy, the cheese pie gets thicker and thicker.

She's our super nana and we think she's cool.
She's our super nana, a fabulous jewel.

She's a big dogaholic, a fab doggy sitter,
Walking the dogs makes her fitter and fitter.
They see her each day but don't seem to care.
It seems they're at home when Nana is there.

She's our super nana and we think she's cool.
She's our super nana, a fabulous jewel.

When we're down in the dumps and have not go our way,
She is always there with a smile and will say;
'Remember the good times and fun times you've had,
playing with Alice, Mum and your dad.'

She's our super nana and we think she's cool.
She's our super nana, a fabulous jewel.

Molly Howarth (9)

My Favourite Person

My favourite person is my sister,
Her name is Abbie but sometimes she annoys me
And I become crabby.

Alanah Kiernan (6)

Nanny Nunn

My favourite person
Is undoubtedly Nanny Nunn.
She's very kind and lovely,
And always lots of fun!

She's sometimes calm,
And hardly ever in a hurry.
She always has
A fuss and a worry.

We like the same things,
Well, most of the time.
For instance, she has the same colour on her bedroom wall,
That I have on mine.

I want her to be there,
For the special things in my life.
I want her to live long enough,
To see me become someone's wife.

When we took her to the zoo,
She could not understand,
How I could hold a cockroach,
In my bare hand.

She's the best nanny anywhere,
She's as smiley as the sun.
Who's my favourite person?
My wonderful Nanny Nunn.

Eleanor Martin (9)

My Bear Fluff

F urry little friend
L ovely to cuddle
U nbearably cute
F un to have around
F ills my heart with joy.

Joseph McKenna (8)

My Favourite Things

I like playing football in the sun
Rugby's entertaining and lots of fun.
Hard work and tiring it can be overall
But good fun comes from running after a ball!

I play the flute a tune a day
From Grade 1 to 3 I can play.
If I play the piano, all the notes I know
I'm not a professional, but I've given it a go!

Being with my mates is so much fun
We can still meet up if there is no sun.
We could talk in a room all day
A game of Truth or Dare we could play!

Spending time with my family I like to do
From going on holiday to visiting a zoo.
Playing in the garden, as happy as can be
But we all calm down when it's time for tea!

My dogs I adore most of all
Taking them walks, playing fetch with a ball.
I give them attention, I know they like that
I couldn't do this if I had a pet bat!

So now you know my favourite things
From football, to pets, to collecting rings.
All those things mean the world to me
Without them who knows where I'd be!

Zoe McConkey (12)

My Favourite Person

My favourite person makes me glad
She's my mum and never sad.
She loves me to the max
I know this, it's a fact.
My mum.

Niamh Porter (9)

No Ordinary Dad

My dad is very special, not like other dads,
He really is an inspiration to all those other lads.
For he has fought for our country on the front line,
He doesn't tell me much about it, but if I ask he doesn't mind.
He trained for six months,
He was out there for six months, that's a whole year.
It must have been nice, because, he's done it twice!
Yes, to Afghanistan and Iraq he went
Too far his mind has bent.
I can't imagine how scary it must have been
And all the horrible things he would have seen.
But in the end he got paid for it
A candle - for once - someone else has lit.
You usually see her on the TV screen
Yes, that's right, my dad visited the Queen!
He was also on TV himself and so was I
Honestly, I'm not kidding, it's not a lie!
He also met Ross Kemp as well.
A photo and an autograph, in my house it does dwell.
For Dad is not going back ever again - never again.
If he did, he would be classed as insane!
I would really like to thank my dad for being the best dad in the world
And even though I'm growing up, I'll still be his little girl.
No one else can imagine, how proud right now I feel
For the fighting out there is not pretend, it's all real.

Cecilia Micklethwaite (12)

My Favourite Person

My best friend is Isobel, I like her a lot.
Every time I look at her, me and her go hippity hop.
She makes me laugh, she makes me cry
She sometimes makes me angry
And I sometimes make her sigh.
Everybody is fair and that's why we all get along.

Shannon Wigley (8)

My Favourite People

Uncle Jay;
Uncle Jay well what can we say?
Up for the 'Boro hooray, hooray,
We went to his house and put holes in his wall
Some were big and some were small.

Uncle Will;
Uncle Will he's so funny,
He lives in a place called Scunny.
He prances around in the air,
As his dreadlocks wave everywhere.

He and uncle Jay bought us a trampoline,
Though me and my Ben were very keen,
To jump up and down and scream,
Will raises his glasses above his eyes,
It make us feel so surprised.
Yes, that's my Uncle Will.

Nana;
I love my nana so much,
I can almost feel her touch.
It was hard to say goodbye.
It made me feel I was going to cry.
I will tell my nana every problem,
So she can help me solve them.

Megan Rose Hopper (10)

Beyoncé

B rilliant talent
E xcellent dancer
Y ou never get bored of her music
O riginal style
N o one can come close
C aring and a good person
E nthusiastic and lively.

Dionne Burgin (9)

My Mother

My mother is full of beauty and grace
She is like a dazzling light just like faith.
She's like the ocean, calm and wavy
Not like what you see in the navy.

She is what you would want her to be
Just like a golden, pretty, smart bee.
She is special as can be
She is also precious to me.

She is colourful and bright
Just like the exceptional Rose light.
She is special to me and my family
She is different with a hint of lovely.

She sets examples to me
So I can be just like a smart bee
I love my mother and she loves me
And I will love her the way I love the rest of my family.
My mother is the candle light
Which brightens our days.

Rose is what my mother is
With a hint of violet and some quiz.
She's kind and nice with laughter and fun
Shining bright like the morning sun.

Christiana Oladokun

My Best Friend Caitlin Wilcox

My best friend loves ponies,
Caitlin is the best,
And she has a sister who she thinks is better than the rest.

She really loves her sister,
Caitlin has owls,
And when I don't see her I miss her,
And she has some pink towels.

Emma Harrison (11)

Leon

Who's my favourite person you ask?
Well you see there's only one person
It could truly be.

He's always been tall,
So he's easy to look up to,
And I guess you could say he's taught me a thing or two.

He makes me laugh,
And he makes me cry,
But I still love him and I haven't a clue why.

Without him I don't know where I'd be,
All I know is . . .
I'd be a completely different me.

He's my hero,
The one I respect the most,
He's in my top ten – like God to the Holy Ghost.

I guess you could say,
I rate him pretty high,
But the thing is, he's just not you're everyday type of guy.

He's what you could call special to me,
He's what you would call my family,
He's what I should call my big brother.

Niccole Matthews (15)

My Favourite Person!

My favourite person is my mum because
She gets things for my tum.
She hugs me, kisses me and makes me
Laugh and helps me with my maths.

When I'm feeling sad my mummy makes me
Glad and never stops loving me.
I love my mum.

Jessica Broughton (9)

My Favourite Person

What is a friend?
A friend is someone you can talk to
And share your feelings with,
Someone who makes you smile,
Tells good jokes and makes you laugh
Whenever you are down, they always make you feel better.

What is a friend?
A friend is someone who is not judgemental,
They like you for who you are,
Whenever you are lonely they are always there to comfort you,
Whenever you are happy, they are happy too.
You have so many things in common that you share.

What is a friend?
A friend is someone who reassures you
And will always listen to the good or bad things
And whenever you disagree or argue, you will
Always manage to make up,
Friends are always kind and understanding.

My friend is Evie,
She is my favourite person,
And I hope we will be friends for life!

Tiahna Joshi (10)

My Little Brother

My little brother is cute,
He eats lots of fruit.
My brother is a laugh,
He loves to have a bath.
My little brother is a shorty,
But he can be very naughty.
My little brother is crazy,
Just like my cousin Maisie.
And that's my little brother.

Kate Brown (12)

My Guinea Pigs

I love my guinea pigs, Daisy and Maisy.

Daisy and Maisy eat all of the time,
Every morning they make me shine.

If they died I would be sad,
Because I'm always happy, it would just be bad!

Sometimes Daisy,
Drives me crazy!

They hardly sleep,
They just eat and eat and eat.

They live in a pigloo,
That looks like an igloo.

They like to play,
And love their hay.

Daisy has red eyes,
She is very wise.

They are both very fat,
Just like my neighbour's cat!

I love Daisy and I love Maisy.

Alexia McGuinness (11)

Mother

My mum is funny
She is full of honey
She is there for me
She cares for me

She is the golden sun
That brightens my day
I will thank her each and every day
She wipes my tears
And now my fears.

Roheen Nawaz (11)

My Favourite Person - Someone Special To Me

David Tennant

David Tennant is really great
He worked with Catherine Tate
He is a wonderful actor
And he has the X factor

If I met him I would blush
And my words would turn to mush
When he's on the TV I smile
And to meet him I would run a mile

David Tennant is thirty-eight
Does anyone know his fate?
He's the greatest Doctor ever
And he is really clever

His TARDIS travels through space and time
To travel with him would be divine
He used to work with Billie Piper
The TARDIS needs a window wiper

When I found out he would leave
I wiped my tears on my sleeve
He is such a great Doctor Who
David Tennant I will really miss you.

Jude Hunt (11)

Barbie (My Pony)

There stood a horse so elegant and beautiful.
Standing so patiently in a stable full of cobwebs.
She took the bit and I slipped on her saddle,
Then I mounted her back
And we rode away.

We rode across the beach into the water.
Her hooves pounding in the golden sand,
Her snow-white mane flowing in the soft wind.
I felt the thrill of her freedom in my hands.

Hannah Smith (12)

My Best Friend Fergus

One blue-eyed, one brown-eyed friend
That was Fergus the dog,
Soft and gentle
But when it came to his food, he turned into a hog.

A coat so white
As white as the snow,
A coat so soft
He's the best dog that I know.

A playful dog
Lively but fun,
With paws 'n' claws
This dog was number one.

But the worst was to come
He soon fell ill,
We never got to say goodbye
But I love him still.

So this poem is a memorial to him
I'll love him until the end,
Goodbye, goodbye, so long, farewell
My furry, brilliant friend.

Amy Nicole Mann (11)

Everyone Is Equal

I don't have a favourite person,
Because I don't want to make a fuss.

I like everyone, good or bad.
Some people do bad things
But inside them is always a good person.
A woman is a woman.
A man is a man.
A boy is a boy,
But everyone is equal.

Josh Miles (11)

My Grumpy Grandad

I have a grumpy grandad who has a curly tash.
He's never used a credit card, he only uses cash.
He hates the rainy British weather, he thinks it's a pain.
That's why he'd much rather go to Spain.

He's married to my nana who's name is Tess
She often wears a pretty dress.
She always brings granddad cups of tea,
But it always hurts her bad knees.

He is always building interesting things
Like jewellery which includes precious rings
He builds wooden animals, such as ducks and goats
And the duck he built actually floats.

He enjoys a cup of good coffee,
But his teeth are too fragile to chew toffee,
His favourite food is gravy, sausage and mash
But he gets it caught in his moustache.

But although he sometimes gets glumpy
And he often gets very mad and grumpy.
He is my special granddad
And he always calls me a good lad.

Issac Cross-Costello (11)

My Best Friend

My best friend is small and white,
Although she is very cute she may sometimes bite,

She fits in the palm of my hand,
But I wouldn't sell her for 100 grand.

My friend is a hamster, Jordan's her name,
But when she is older, she will have fame.

Jordan's very sad now because she made a den
But then we took the wheel away, so she has to make it again.

Maddison Rourke (8)

Usain Bolt

He hails from Jamaica,
The island in the sea,
When asked, 'How so fast?'
He answered, 'Rice and peas.'

Beijing was the site,
When a star was born,
He won the hundred metres,
He took the world by storm.

He didn't finish there,
He took the two, easy,
Smashed world records,
And came back for the relay.

He came to Berlin
He never lost his smile,
He repeated 2008 glory,
Beat the rest by a mile.

He is a superstar,
No athlete can cope,
The fastest man alive,
Usain 'lightning' Bolt.

Emma Dunbar (11)

My Big Sister

My best friend, oh how do I start,
Movies, ice cream, us looking the part,
'Stardust' and 'Wild Child' then Nando's too,
Borders and Jessops and then gigs too,
Oh yes, I've saved the best till last
Erdigg Hall where we had a blast,
Horses and sneezes and hospitals too,
You were there for them all that's why
I love you.

Emily Rose Tweedale (12)

All My Favourite People!

I've lots of favourite people
And this I'll tell you why
Each of them has got a reason
To always make me smile.

My mum makes me yummy food
My dad takes me out
My sisters love to tickle me
Until I kick and shout!

Mrs Tunkel (that's my teacher)
Gives me lots of rewards
When I'm feeling poorly
The doctor opens her doors!

My best friend Talia
Tells such awful jokes
Then there's Faye and Serena
Who always gives me a poke!

When I'm feeling down
Or maybe a little feeble
I know they'll come to my rescue
'cause they're my favourite people!

Adaeze Ebodili (11)

My Mum

My mum is great, she buys me
Lots and lots from the shops.
My mum is always happy
And kind and she is pretty.
She is always going to work
To get lots of pennies for me.
My mum always makes me laugh
Because she is so funny
And I love her lots and lots.

Jessica Ellis

My Cousin Liam

My cousin Liam
Is the best
He lives near me
At Slyne-with-Hest.

His friend Charlie
She's quite great
Even though
She's only eight.

Then there's Ethan
What a laugh
The only trouble
He doesn't bath.

His sister Courtney
Loves to draw
But she's definitely
Not a real big bore.

They're all Liam's friends
Aren't they ace?
I hope this poem's
Put a smile on your face.

Sam Davidson-Pennington (11)

My Favourite Person

My favourite person is so sweet,
She doesn't care if I have stinky feet.
I think of one word, she is mad, but think of another word
Because when she is with me I am glad,
She wouldn't kick me out the door,
Just because I didn't hoover the floor,
She tucks me in so I fall asleep and the wish I have I keep,
My favourite person is my mum, she and I together
We are not dumb, we just want to lie under the sun.

Susie Concannon (11)

Jenny Scott!

I have got more than one favourite person,
My family, friends and celebs are all great,
But Jenny Scott is my best friend,
But I've only known her since I was eight!

Jenny stood out more than all the others,
I just knew that we would be friends!
She is so kind, helpful and funny,
Our friendship will never end.

We are always together at school -
No one can tear us apart!
We always laugh and have lots of fun,
As a friend I love her with all my heart.

When anyone ever sees me,
Jenny is by my side.
In the playground, anywhere else,
I would never leave her behind.

Jenny Scott is my best friend,
Never are we not together.
She will be in future, she is now,
Forever and ever.

Rebecca Emma Guy (10)

My Best Friend Antonia

We've had so many good times together
No matter where we are, even in the sewer
Or sitting in the car
I reached out to this friend
To show her how much I care
To pull her close and let her know
Just how much I need her there
If ever I'm in pain, she'll stop the rain
To put sunshine above my head.

Chloe Collins (11)

Izzy

I have a friend called Izzy,
I like her very much,
She's never very busy,
So we always keep in touch.

I have a friend called Izzy,
I think she's very cool,
She always makes me laugh,
Even when we are at school.

I have a friend called Izzy,
She is my best friend,
I know we'll be together,
'Til the very end.

I have a friend called Izzy,
She's someone I can trust,
She keeps my secrets safe,
To tell her is a must.

My favourite person is Izzy,
And you know why,
I know you'll really like her,
And that is not a lie!

Alice Mason (10)

My Favourite Person

My favourite person is always there for me even when he's watching TV
My favourite person is very strong but never wrong
My favourite person has black hair and is very fair
My favourite person is tall not small and called Paul
My favourite person likes to eat cheese but has dodgy knees
My favourite person has got green eyes and likes pork pies
My favourite person is the best and beats the rest
My favourite person is my dad
And he is *fab*!

Kate Appleton (11)

My Favourite Person Amelia

There's a lot of people that I love,
They're so good and kind,
They should go to Heaven above,
That's what goes on in my mind.

I'll start off with my school friends,
There will be no end,
And even when our friendship bends,
It's sure to re-mend.

Next there are my toys,
I love them all to bits,
But I can make a lot of noise,
To me they're all a hit.

Then there is my family,
They are all the best!
I know they will still love me,
Even when I am a pest!

But my favourite person is,
My fab and loving sister,
And when she went to PGL,
I well and truly missed her!

Grace Richards (10)

My Granny

Her smile can light up a room,
Her presence is of grace,
Her opinions are heard without one word but by the look upon her face,
Her touch is so gentle, her heart as big as the moon,
Her spirit is kind-hearted and warm as a summer's afternoon,
Her hair a river of grey, her eyes radiant as the sun,
Her time she'll take no matter how long, until the work is done,
Her kisses are so soft, her hugs preferred from the rest,
My granny is mine forever and ever, and she'll always be the best.

Clara Kevin (11)

If My Mum Were . . .

If my mum were in the Olympics
She'd win first place in washing, ironing and cooking.
She does it all for me
I love my mum.
If my mum were the Queen
The first thing she would do
Is make every day a Mummy Day
I love my mum.
If my mum were a shooting star
She would be the brightest star there
I love my mum.
If my mum were a butterfly
She would be the most elegant creature
In the animal kingdom
I love my mum.
If my mum were me
She'd be cool, funky and fashionable!
I love my mum.
If my mum were my mum . . .
Oh yes she is!
Lucky me.

Naomi Wrigley (10)

Super Mum

Most people would say their mum's the best,
But I have to disagree because mine is,
Caring and loving, fun and serious all at the same time
My mum really is a great mum.

She takes me places when no one else can
She always buys me ice cream.
But when I misbehave, I have got to be punished
But I know she is only doing her job.
But through all of this there is only one way to describe my mum,
She is like a super mum.

Emma Kennedy (10)

Uncle George

My favourite person is Uncle George
Because he took me on holiday in the van
And also has a dog named Sam.
We went on a roller coaster
We really did scream
And after that we had ice cream.
He beat daddy on the go-karts
That was so cool
He even took me swimming
In the big pool.
Uncle George really is the best
A cut above all the rest
He took me on holiday
The safari park too
That's something I always wanted to do.
When he visits me
It's always fun
He makes me laugh
He loves me a lot
That's why he's my favourite person
And granny is not.

Jemma McIvor (6)

My Favourite Person Is . . .

Grandad you are wonderful
You always make me smile
I'll see you in a little while
You like chocolate just like me
Now just have a cup of tea
Look in my eyes, you can see
I'm going to laugh, *he, he, he* . . .
Just one more thing, I am your princess
And I always will be.

I love you grandad.

Sophia Hume (10)

My Mum

She takes me to school.
Taught me to swim,
In a freezing cold pool.
She keeps me healthy,
Talks to me when I'm sad.
Buys me birthday presents,
And never gets mad.

She takes me shopping,
Gives me fashion advice.
In exchange for that,
I'm very nice,
Sometimes we do,
Drive each other crazy.
Like when I don't do my homework,
Because I'm being lazy!

But no matter what we do,
I know that I love her,
Not because she gives me pocket money,
But because . . . she's my mother,
And I love her!

Erin Thompson (10)

Nanny

She cooks and cleans for me
She is my queen
Nanny loves me no matter what
And looks after me when I'm hot
When I'm hurt she makes it better
She helps me write my letters
When I'm good and when I'm bad
She loves me still and that makes me glad
I love Nanny, she's the best
And I love her more than all the rest.

Crystal Daniels (6)

My Mother

She is the best,
She's better than the rest,
I could ask for no other.

She likes to go on walks,
She also likes to talk,
I am talking about my mother.

She is the greatest ever,
She seldom loses her tether,
I couldn't want another.

She is very caring,
But isn't very daring,
I am talking about my mother.

She is very kind,
The most honest person you could find,
I could ask for no other.

She really likes flowers,
But doesn't have powers,
She's just naturally the most phenomenal mother.

Christopher Bentley (10)

My Mum

My mum is the best.
She does the best dinners in the world
And my mum is aged 29.

My mum has glasses
And works in the post office in Wantage.

My mum's eyes are green
And Mum's favourite colour is purple.
She gives me a kiss and hug.

Mum has a boyfriend called Phil
Who plays football.

Eryn Lamble (10)

Cora Is The One

There are more than one hundred ways to describe my friend.
I want our friendship to never end.

You help me when I'm stuck,
No need to scream and shout,
You're always there without a doubt.

Our sleepovers are fun,
We watch movies at night,
Eat popcorn in the bedroom,
Until it's time to turn out the light.

You're the one who cheers me up when
I'm sad and down,
Without you, on my face there would be a frown.

She never misses her school or mass,
I love Cora she's so class.

I love Cora she's the one that I have been looking for,
She sticks up for me,
The lock to our friendship will
Have the key.

Lauren McComb (10)

My Hamster Theodore

My hamster, Theodore, is very, very silly
He sits in the food bowl while eating his meals.
He is so, so silly that the other night
He piled up all the sawdust to the top of his wheel.
Theodore likes to go around the house every night
He runs around in his ball.
He can always find his way to the kitchen
But he sometimes bumps into the wall.
When he is running in his wheel
He really makes me giggle
Because when he's running, his buttocks wiggle.

Jasmine Cargan (10)

My Pal

My pal is tri-coloured, white, black with brown,
White with black spots, brown around his mouth,
His fur is soft like velvet,
Eyes shining like bronze stars lit up in the large midnight sky,
Moist wet nose, short waggy tail,
I play with him lots to pass the time by,
With his small little legs he can run quite fast,
I can't keep up with my mischievous old pal,
His legs don't lift him far off the ground,
We are opposites, he is small and I am tall,
He loves hunting for rats,
Me helping too, walks down the field he stops for a . . .
Running through the muddy puddles,
Me splashing, running up behind,
We have such fun he is so cute,
He's really good company,
By the time we get home my pal needs some fuel,
Food for my pal, some for my too,
Can you guess who my pal is?
Oh by the way, his name is Kipper, does that give you a clue?

Hannah Boniface (12)

Best Friends

B uddies love to share everything.
E very holiday we meet up at least once.
S weets, of course, we love to share at midnight.
T esting each other on various things is fun

F riends are a complete pleasure to have,
R ough and tumble, we love it!
I have quite a few best friends.
E very day we laugh and play with smiles on our faces.
N o one knows my best friends - *top secret!*
D odging balls, on the trampoline, jumping high as we go.
S chool, the No 1 place to make friends.

Charlotte Clews (10)

Santa Claus

He dresses up all in fur, from his head to his foot,
And his clothes are all tarnished, with ashes and soot;
He has a bundle of toys flung on his back,
And looks like a peddler just opening his pack
His eyes, how they twinkle, his dimples, how merry!
His cheeks are like roses, his nose like a cherry!
His droll little mouth is drawn up like a bow,
And the beard on his chin is as white as snow;
The stump of a pipe, he holds tight in his teeth,
And the smoke, it encircles his head like a wreath;
He has a broad face and a little round belly,
That shakes when he laughs, like a bowl full of jelly,
He is chubby and plump, like his old jolly self,
I laugh when I see him on telly, in spite of myself;
He speaks not a word, but goes straight to work,
And fills houses with presents, then turns with a jerk.
He springs to his sleigh, and gives his team a whistle,
And away they fly, like the down of a thistle.
But yet I think I smell his steam,
But it always turns out to be a magical dream.

Majidah Begum (9)

The Old Man

The old man
Is my favourite person
He is eighty-four with ginger hair.
His eyes shimmer and never grow dimmer
He keeps going even though he is not growing
He loves to be around me when we are both in glee
And I love him, like he loves me.

The old man
Is my loyal companion,
My dog,
And Lionel is my favourite person.

Charlie Rogers-Smith (11)

My Inspirational Teacher

A rainbow of dazzling colours,
Lighting up my day!
When I have lost my smile,
We search for it together.
My favourite teacher would never,
Give up.

Helping me find my feet,
When I land the wrong way.
Loving and caring,
Happy and sharing.
Where am I?
In the dark she will
Turn on the light.

But when I take my first steps,
On to the path named *future*,
I will never forget her.
She is a glistening
Bubble in my memory,
That will never pop . . .

Imogen Daisy Clay (10)

Smudge

Smudge is a cat who stays
Round my grandma's
The cat that went missing
When I see him he always wants to play
So I tease him with long grass in my grandma's garden
His owners live up the road and they don't see him in the day
I once heard him burp and because he's a cat he didn't say pardon

Smudge is a cat who is friendly, he licks you all over
He loves to eat meat and nick Brandy's food
I missed him when I went to Dover
Once I stroked him after he had just pooed.

Thomas Peters

My Favourite Person - My Mum

There's this woman I will always love,
She's like my angel from above,
She is my guardian angel who will always be
A very special part of me.

I call this woman my mum, she's very special to me,
She's everything any child would want their mum to be.
I know she loves me by the way she shows me care.
She hugs me and talks to me, when I need her, she's always there.

My life would not be complete without my mum, my best friend,
I know she'll always be here, until the very end.
I've grown up so fast, but I'll always be her baby girl forever,
As I love every single minute we spend together.

We've had so many memories, they've all been so good,
She cares for me, is kind to me, she showers me with love.
My mum, she's my world, she's everything to me,
She's made me the best that I could ever be!

I'd like to say thank you for all that she's done,
She's my life support, my everything, that woman I call my mum!

Jessica Peers (13)

My Big Brother

My big brother is so cool,
I always talk about him at school.

My big brother is so strong,
He's always right and never wrong.

My big brother is so tall,
He's the best at football.

My big brother is so smart,
And he is so good at art.

Now you know a bit about my brother,
You can see that he's better than others!

Amina Miah (11)

My Sis Is Bliss

My sis is bliss,
She's lovely, she's pretty
So you don't want to miss
Her lovely kiss.

She's the best friend you could have
She's fun and caring.
She's a treasure to keep.

My sis is bliss
She's lovely, she's pretty
So you don't want to miss
Her lovely kiss.

She's gorgeous, she's super
She's sweet as sugar
She's a dream come true.

Sometimes we fight
Sometimes we don't get along
But I love and treasure her
Because, my sis is bliss!

Katie Quirk (9)

My Dad

My dad is the best,
I think he is better than the rest.

My dad takes me for a ride,
When we play football he is on my side.

He's good on computers, he plays guitar,
I think my dad is a star.

He's good at cards but not as good as me,
Who will win tonight? We'll have to wait and see.

Chocolate is his favourite treat,
You wouldn't believe how much he can eat!

Jenny Law (7)

Mary King

Top horse rider Mary King,
Is good at everything
To do with horses and courses,
And horsy fashion things.

Her horses are fast,
They're such a blast,
Galloping and trotting
With every swing.

She's so cool, she rules,
She has got funny hair,
But I don't care.

I would love to be her,
For she is so cool,
If I copy her
I might not fall!

And that is my favourite person,
Mary King
Number one horse riding legend!

Georgia Clark (10)

My Grandad (My Special Person 2009)

I would enter my special person's house and the first thing he would say is,
'Ay up lass, are you OK?'

He would then grab me and squeeze me with his big strong arms,
And carry on welcoming me with his slang Yorkshire charm.

My southern accent would come over strange,
As speaking this way is not in his range.

We would then sit down, and be relaxing
When he would suddenly start singing.

At the end of the day, he would put down his mug
And never miss out on our goodbye hug.

Louise Firth (11)

My Favourite Person

My favourite person is my dad,
He is the funniest dad in the world because he can flare
His nostrils like an ugly dragon.
When he tickles me with his scratchy whiskers
It makes me laugh 'til my belly hurts.

My favourite person is my dad,
He is the sportiest dad in the world because
He passes a rugby ball to me,
Bowls a cricket ball at me,
Plays tennis with me,
And goes jogging with me.

My favourite person is my dad,
He is the strongest dad in the world
Because he pins me to the ground when we play wrestling.
In thumb wars he lets me nearly win and then suddenly
Crushes my small thumb with his mighty thumb.

My favourite person is my dad
He is the best dad in the world because he's mine!

Jack Elliot Culver (10)

My Favourite Person

You are the one that makes me smile every day,
By giving me advice that I'll always remember,
Cooking and caring for me when I'm ill,
Cheering me up when I'm down,
Helping me when I'm stuck,
All year round you do these things and don't moan a bit,
If you stopped doing the things that you do,
Everything would come to a standstill,
If I fell apart you would be the one to put my pieces back together,
I don't know what I'd do without you,
You are my favourite person,
You are my *mum!*

Ryan Howitt (11)

My Gran

Nana:
Your smile beams,
Face glows,
Your love for me,
Is always shown!

Your radiance flows,
Your scent stays,
The tears in my eyes,
Soon dry away.

Your face is soft,
With hands of silk,
Your cooking is sweet,
Biscuits and milk!

Your tears are unseen,
Cries unheard,
You're the essence of love.
Red, to purple, orange then pink.
Sometimes green, but never blue.

Maya Sharda

When I Am With My Grandad

My grandad loves watching boxing.
But, when he is with me, we watch Disney.
I love my grandad, he is my best friend.
When he teases me about boyfriends,
He drives me round the bend.
I tell grandad all of my secrets and
I trust him.
Grandad is kind.
Grandad never breaks a promise.
He spends time with me at Christmas.
He plays lots of games and tells funny jokes.
My grandad is the best!

Ellie Farmer (12)

My Favourite Person!

There is one special lad,
Who happens to be my dad.
He is very thoughtful and caring,
Although he gets a bit mental
When he starts swearing.
But that's because he has to put up with me
And my two annoying sisters, Karina and Phoebe.
I'm his favourite, that's something he can't deny,
He just won't admit it, I don't know why!
But let's get back to my dad, yes the one that's turning grey,
But to be honest, he's the one to always save the day.
If he's not walking or working, he's helping out,
It wouldn't be the same without him – no doubt!
He might have to nag and nag,
Until he eventually loses his rag.
But he's always happy to give us money,
Always making people laugh, being funny.
But the best thing is, yes even better than beer,
Is that everything is perfect as long as my dad is here!

Katie Clarke (13)

My Dog Tigger

My dog is called Tigger.
I'd like him much bigger.
He lies in bed with his tongue sticking out,
With one ear up and one ear down.

If we put make-up on him,
He would look like a clown.
He loves the outdoors and going for walks.
He chews his bone and barks at the phone.
He goes to the Poodle Parlour to get his fur cut.
When he is finished he's the most handsome mutt.
I love him, I love him, he is my best friend.
I love him so much, now this is the end.

Matilda Burnie (8)

My Papa

My papa is great
He thinks he's twenty-eight

I won't reveal his real age
His face will turn beige

He takes us to loads of places
Crazy, wide and open spaces

If you have a problem, call his phone
You'll end up in the chill-out zone

He buys stuff at the bakery Heatherlea
For Mum, Dad, Guy the dog and me

Wherever he goes he can't help treating us
When he takes us home on the bus

We would have ice creams, chocolate, or packets of sweets
These are my favourite treats

So thank you Papa for looking after me
I'll pay you back sometime . . . you'll see.

Zoë Elena Beckett (11)

Hannah

Hannah is my best friend,
She's been with me till the end
Someone I can rely on.
She is a special one
An excellent secret keeper
And definitely a weeper.

We have had fallouts like friends do
But make up with a surprising, *'Boo'*
A fun, wicked, jokey friend
I hope we're friends to the end
Loves gravy like me
We were just meant to be!

Grace Bird (10)

First Day Back

It's the first day back at school,
Floors are sparkling,
Teachers are back to marking.

It's the first day back at school,
I'm in a new class,
With my flask,
Ready to go to lunch.

It's the first day back at school,
Primary 1's are crying,
Mums are fed up buying.

Brand new uniforms, bright and green,
We're all ready
'Cause it's the first day back at school.

It's the first day back at school,
Wow, my teacher's nice,
With a voice as cool as ice,
Because it's the first day back.

Lauren Fiddes (10)

My Friends

S omething in common with me
H er hair is long and very long
A good friend to me
N eeds to stop biting her fingernails
I n trouble all the time
A ctive and very alive

T ogether all the time
E xcellent manners
G ood at dancing
A good friend
I mportant to me
N eeds to stop shouting and fighting with Shania.

Casey Haslam (10)

My Friend Gemma

Gemma's my best friend,
And we'll be friends to the end.
Here are the reasons why,
Gemma can be shy,
Always honest and true,
A real friend for me and you.
Always there to lend a hand,
When things don't go to plan.
Gemma is so funny,
Even when it's not sunny.
She always lights up my day,
In her own peculiar way.
Gemma is by far,
A true shining star.
With her golden hair and eyes of blue,
She's pretty, she is too.

And now you know why,
My favourite person is my best friend Gemma.

Leah Lafferty (10)

My Little Sister Rosie

My little sister Rosie is a burst of energy waiting to explode.
She is a mischievous kitten with a ball of wool.
She's a three-year-old with a heart of gold and the face of an angel.
Rosie is like a chocolate cake that's only been half eaten.
She's a sneaky magpie who's discovered a sparkling necklace.
Rosie's always summer, never winter.
In the morning she's a bouncy spring with wide beady eyes
Jumping around even though we're all still drowsy.
Rosie is a skippy lamb, bright and cheerful.
She is a delicate snowflake dancing in the breeze.
She is a surprise present waiting to be opened
But most importantly Rosie is my little sister
And I love her very much.

Alice Payne (10)

Miley Cyrus

In late November 1992,
In Franklin, Tennessee,
My favourite ever star was born,
And she was named Miley.

Long blond hair,
And rockin' moves,
For me she can't go wrong,
I love her outfits and her looks,
But most of all her songs!

I wish she lived much closer,
And we could have a ball,
Forget Pop Idol and X Factor,
As Miley has it all.

Miley Cyrus is her name,
But don't write that on your banner,
As when she's dressed for rockin' out,
She's known as *Hannah Montana!*

Emily Wilson (10)

Sir Alan Sugar

He has a great business mind
He can or cannot be kind
He can make or break you
Not to mention a few
He is my idol
My person that I most admire
He is the one who was inspiring
He is my idol, my favourite person
He is Sir Alan Sugar
A great businessman
With a great business mind
He drove me to love doing business
That's why I love him.

Lauren Gibson (13)

My Favourite Person

Even though I've known her all my life,
I couldn't say I know her well,
I may think I do,
But I know there's more that she keeps hidden.

She can be happy, sweet and nice,
But everyone has two sides,
She's hard to predict,
She could be fierce, selfish or as cold and hard as ice.

No matter how hard she hides herself,
She knows that I will find her,
And no matter how much she mixes herself up,
She knows that I will solve her.

It's hard to say why she's my favourite person,
But I think it's because I can trust her,
Or because no matter how she feels I know she would never hurt me,
No matter how much we bicker and fight,
My favourite person will always be my sister.

Georgie McKenzie Smith (11)

My Favourite Person

My favourite person means the world to me
My favourite person is my mum
She means a lot as she loves, cares and cooks for me
I help my mum because she helps me
She keeps me safe in a wonderful home
It's very clean and tidy
I'm always up early for school in the morning
My mum always makes sure I am home safe
With my mum I'm never sad
I feel so wanted with my family, especially my mum
I'm so glad to know that I am wanted by someone
Who is so special and someone who I love
My mum, my favourite person in the world.

Venus MacKenzie (10)

My Best Friend!

In the paddock he runs,
Towards me he comes,
His fur as soft as velvet,
Mane blowing in the wind,
How carefully he stops.

I give him an apple,
He takes it from my hand,
'Neigh, neigh,' he says,
as delightful as it sounds,
I brush him with a curry comb,
I wish he lived in my home.

I ride him through the forest,
I feel like I'm the tallest,
Over the fallen tree trunk he goes,
Nobody knows where he likes to go,
But I do,
He's my best friend, Arty!

Hannah Rusling (12)

She Is A Star

This is a caring person
She is a star
She wears glasses
She owns a million cars
She is pretty
She is a star
But she goes on, *bla, bla, bla*
She is eleven
I am eight
She always stands up straight
We both like dancing
My friend is my cousin
One more time, she is a star!

Bethanie Mortenson (8)

Usain Bolt

My favourite person is the king of cool
He makes everybody else look like a fool
He has won loads of races and,
His name is Usain Bolt!

Bolt took part in Beijing
And Berlin (so far)
He broke world records
And won loads of bling (gold medals)

My favourite person is the king of cool
He makes everybody else look like a fool
He has won loads of races and,
His name is Usain Bolt.

Bolt is a nice, serious
And friendly guy
No wonder people love
To see him racing by.

Luke McCarron (10)

My Friend Ben

I have many friends whom I like
They play with me whilst I ride my bike.

My favourite one is a boy called Ben
He is the same age as me, he is ten.

We have lots of fun and laugh together
Even when it's nasty, rainy weather.

We roller skate and kick our ball
Our neighbour gets cross when it goes over her wall.

Friends are special, a lot to me
We never argue and we play as three.

I would love to win at 'Toys 'R' Us'
We go there sometimes on the bus.

Harry Thewlis (10)

Untitled

My idol is Ryan Giggs,
Man U's magic on the wing
he has a lot of skills,
and he makes all the fans sing.

Sure Giggsy might be old,
but he's still good nonetheless
and it's plainly clear to me
he's still, no doubt, the best.

So his best time may be passed,
he was top for a while
but it's obvious to me,
he's still got a lot of style.

So come on everybody,
why can't you see?
that he is the king of football,
come on Giggsee!

Ryan McMahon (11)

Edward Cullen

My love is as cold as an icy stone,
but forever he will be beside me,
his voice is as soft as a baritone,
now everything can be eternally free.
His topaz eyes shimmer like the sunset,
his beauty dazzles everyone in sight,
for his beauty creates deep despair yet,
he clenches his hand into mine so tight.
His deep topaz eyes are desirable,
but his bronze hair is deeply beautiful,
to me, he is always so valuable,
I remember him as so wonderful.
He is and always will be my deep love,
and nothing is stronger than our love.

Aimee May Walker (13)

Heidi

My little sister Heidi,
Is very rarely tidy,
And when she screams,
It thunders through my ears.

Her tummy is as chubby,
As one of the Teletubbies.
And she hates it when
I try to brush her curly hair.

She is so much fun,
Her blue eyes sparkle like the sun.
And when she laughs,
It makes me feel warm inside.

She's a little cheeky monkey,
But I think she's rather funky,
And I'll adore her
For the rest of my life.

Tasharna Patrick (12)

My Favourite Person

Sally is a dog,
Who eats so many logs.
She can run very far,
Almost like a shooting star.
When people walk past our lane,
She barks like she's insane.
She is the silliest dog I've every seen,
But she will never be mean.
She ate Daddy's brush,
But had to run in a rush.
We have to plead,
Just to get her on her lead.
If she's annoyed she will defend,
But, Sally is still my friend.

Carla McKeagney (9)

My Favourite Person

My favourite person is my mum
She's really quite a star
She helps me with almost everything
She's the greatest by far

My mummy is active
She's as busy as a bee
Even if she's cross sometimes
She still loves me

My mummy is loving
And very, very kind
She stands out
She's easy to find

I love my mummy
And she loves me
Together we make
A happy family.

Olivia Mailey (11)

What My Mum Means To Me

A mum's love is very rare,
We should all be aware,
Even though she screams and shouts,
I never get what she's on about,
I'm sure I'll know one day when I'm all old, wrinkly and grey.
I know we have our ups and downs,
But my mum can turn things all around.
I figure she means well and good,
Even when I don't behave as I should.
She will always have a special chamber in my heart
Because she is the most precious part.
Mum always wants the best for me,
So I guess it's no mystery,
What my mum means to me.

Alice Talbot (11)

I Don't Have To Choose

My favourite people,
Who do I choose?
Meggy or Jessy,
I'm totally confused.

We travel to school every day,
And when we're not working
We go out to play.

When I'm happy or sad,
They listen to me,
Without my friends,
Where would I be?

The answer is clear,
Two friends are the best,
For friends are forever,
And I'm happy to say,
That's how things will be.

Emily Tullett (10)

My Big Sister

My big sister is my favourite person in the whole world.
Because she gives me money
When I don't have any or don't have enough.
She helps me do my homework when I get stuck.
She plays with me all the time.
She holds my hand when we go on scary rides
But that's more for her.
She tells me all her secrets and I tell her mine.
She lets me hang round with friends.
I'm glad that she is my sister and no one else's.
She's hardly ever mean and she gives me sweets
When she's got some.
She laughs even when I know I made a terrible joke.
This is why she is my favourite person in the whole wide world.

Jennifer Irwin (11)

My Baby Brother

My baby bro
Is so cute,
If I were a pirate
He'd be my loot.

His name is Gerard
I love him so much,
He is only one
But I love him so much.

We love him but
He is a rascal you see
He hides from you
And turns off the TV.

His nickname's nigglesnoosh
Couldn't think of another.
That's why my favourite person
Is my baby brother.

Courtney Green (11)

My Sister And Me

Me and my sister Stacy go lots of places
We even compete in running races
Even although I always lose
I am the one she will always choose
We like to go to candy shops
And our favourite sweet is lollipops
Every day we go to a different place
And then we practise on the running race
For once in my life I actually won
And it was really quite fun
We love to do things together
And we will love each other forever
Stacy is my one and only friend
And we will be together until the end.

Ami Paterson (10)

My Hamster

When I saw her in the pet shop,
My eyes were flooding with love,
I had a certain urge to buy her,
She was no less beautiful than a dove.

When she crawled inside her cage,
She headed straight to her new fluffy bed,
However, when nightfall approached,
She began dancing on her head.

She loved her squeaky green wheel,
But she often slept in there.
I loved when she stood on her tiny hind legs,
And started grooming her lovely hair.

Cleaning her cage was one thing,
Caring for her was another,
And now I can honestly say,
That my hamster was no bother.

Blair Gibson (11)

Miss S Baum!

Miss Baum is my favourite teacher,
I was so lucky to meet her!
She is like my favourite sister I never had,
When I turn up to her lessons I'm always glad!
I really hope you get to see her one day,
What she would think of you I could not say!
Majority of my work is up on the classroom wall,
If anything happens - she said come and call!
There is definitely no other person like Sarah,
And if she wasn't a teacher she would be an amazing carer!
I would say I'm her favourite student in the class,
We could just sit and talk all day on the grass!
So now it is time for my story to end,
If I knew her address there would be millions of letters to send!

Shannon Louise Smith (12)

Mum Is My Chum

I love my mum,
So gorgeous and sweet,
I take care of her,
When she has swollen feet.

She takes me to school,
To and fro
To learn lots of things
Like not to throw.

When I am at school,
I think about her,
Sitting next to the rabbit,
Stroking its fur.

When she picks me up,
She has a smile on her face,
That is my mum,
She's not a disgrace.

Austen Lowe (12)

A Busy Bee

My mum is cool,
But she has too many rules.
She wears this hat,
When she uses the cricket bat.

She loves to sing,
Only if someone joins in.
She's a busy bee,
But she doesn't work out on the Wii,
Because it will always ask, 'Where is she?'

My mum's a workaholic,
But listen, she isn't an alcoholic!
So after writing all this I'm choosing
My mum as my favourite person!

Jasmine Azaei (11)

My Puppy CJ

I've got a dog
She is never sad
She's never naughty
Or never bad

She likes me
She like my mum
She likes getting tickled
On her tum

She likes getting cuddled
And likes to play
She likes her food
And eats all day

She has a cute face
She wants my tea
She looks like a teddy bear
And she loves me.

Callum O'Shaugnessy (9)

Furry Friend

Though Gran's dog's not human
Though she's not young in years
Her nose is wet
She's a great pet
With small tufts at the ends of her ears.

She's named after a small white flower that grows on yonder hill
She's old but healthy
Wise not wealthy
And is hardly ever ill.

So you might think she's useless
And she's as dumb as a log
But to me, well you see,
Daisy's my favourite dog.

Indira Fernando (11)

My Favourite Person

This question is easy,
Easy for me,
Jade is the answer,
My best friend, you see.

We're always together,
Like Siamese twins,
Sharing our secrets,
Sharing our sins.

We look so alike,
Our mum's say we do,
Our height, our hair,
Our button noses too.

Some lucky people get a great friend,
I've got a few,
But my favourite person?
Jade that's you!

Melissa Morton (10)

A True Sister For Life

A true sister is always there for you,
Even in times when you're feeling upset, angry or anxious.
OK yeah, we fight sometimes,
But what matters is we love each other,
No one can stop us from staying the best of friends and sisters,
All the funny times we shared will never be forgotten,
For the times we laughed together so much we couldn't breathe,
For the secrets we shared,
For the fun yet childish times in our room,
To the awful times when we argued.
I thank God for a loving sister,
For a sister is God's way of proving he doesn't want me
to walk alone.

Mabel Osejindu (15)

My Favourite Person

She's like a ray of sunshine,
When nothing but rain fell;
And when I'm feeling sad and blue,
All my troubles I will tell.

She's like an everlasting flower,
A daisy that I once chose;
She's my best friend worthy all over,
From her head down to her toes.

I had no friends in my village,
But when she came at the end of the day;
She asked to be my friend and said,
It's something I've been meaning to say . . .

And from that day we don't really know how,
But a friendship came out of the blue;
We've been best buddies for more than a year,
And kind of like sisters too!

Esme Challis (10)

Arnold Schwarzenegger

Arnold Schwarzenegger is such a good actor,
I don't know why, he's just got the it factor.
If I met him
I would scream,
'Arnold Schwarzenegger, am I in a dream?'
He would pinch me and I would see
It was real,
A novelty.
That night I would think,
Oh my God, I need a drink,
Before I left my dark, damp room,
I would turn to my bed,
'I'll be back . . .'

Dominic Leake (10)

My Mum

My mum, a kindly gentle soul,
Always in some way helping us all,
Her love so tender, her hug so bliss,
Every day I'm wakened by her warming kiss.

No need to question mum, she is always at hand,
Geography homework, she will sort out the land,
Maths, English, and science too,
There is nothing in the world my mum can't do.

Roller coasters are my mum's type of fun,
Always playing with everyone,
Ice skating, bowling, never stopping at all,
Overall my mum's really cool.

I love my mum as you can hear,
She loves me too, she treats me dear,
She helps us all, a gentle dove,
I will never forget her because of her love.

Benjamin Harris (11)

My Mum Left Home

My mum left home when I was five,
She went to live in London.
She's now moved in with a man called Clive
And never sends postcards any more.

I live with my dad,
No money to spare,
We can't even afford,
A ticket to the fair!

My age is ten,
Mum's been gone for five years.
I've kind of forgotten what she looks like now,
But do I really care?

Josephine Gibbs (8)

Who Is . . . ?

Who's the person I get along with?
When I see him he makes me smile
The one I share so many adventures with . . .
And ride our bikes together for a mile!

Who's the person I play with?
I have fun with every day?
Who has very good manners?
But does not always say, 'S'il vous plait.'

He could tell the time before me
He could climb the garden fence
And by the way, 's'il vous plait', three lines above,
Is how you say 'please' in French!

Who was the second child to come?
Who I have loved since I was three
Why it has to be my eight-year-old brother Garnet!
Who is my favourite person you see!

Madeline Charlemagne (11)

My Brother Ciaran

My brother is great
He is a real good mate
We like to play
Almost every day

Cheese is his favourite food
He is always in a good mood
He is always happy but sometimes sad
We cheer him up to make him glad

He's always on his computer
Nearly every day
We can't get him off there
Even if we say.

Caitlin Devenney (10)

Blast-Off

One small step for man
Is one giant leap for mankind.
The humble and determined
Neil Armstrong, one of a kind.

We can only wait and pray
For the ecstatic feeling when he reaches the moon.
We all look up to him,
Emotions strewn.

For so long he'll be my idol
His eyes a shimmer of hope
Encouraging you to be like him
I look up to him like the Pope.

Neil Armstrong the famous
Neil Armstrong never forgotten
He's the humble
And the one and only astronaut.

Anas Aboukoure (9)

Time To Tell You

It's hard to say without letting you know,
Without you, I'd have nowhere to go,
I need you to be there, my friend forever and always,
So that I can be myself and have at least a few happy days.

So many times in the past you've saved me,
Just because I know how disappointed you'd be,
If I ever gave up on you, but that will never come to be,
Because when I'm with you, can't be anything but happy.

So, in case you hadn't guessed, I love you,
And surprisingly enough, I think you love me too,
How I came to have a best friend that will never fade,
Is thanks to the always loving, perfect Jade.

Megan Paul (15)

My Budgie

One gloomy evening my budgie Sam was flying around the room.
He kept landing on my head, then my dad's, then my mum's.
About half an hour after, I put him in his cage.
He is one year old and loves to fly.
He goes mad when my dad goes out of the room
Because my dad's always playing with him
And he doesn't want to stop playing.
When my dad comes back into the room he flies on his head
To try and get him to play again.
When my dad has something to eat, Sam always wants it.
Sam always eats it for him.
Then saves it for my dad in his pouch to have
Because Sam likes to feed my dad.
When he's given him the food that my dad's given him,
He goes and gets his budgie seed and feeds it to him.
He's so cute.
I love him.

Leanne Cooper (10)

My Fantastic Cat

My cat is called Bobby
And chasing flies is his hobby
He just always wants to go out and play
And he miaows when he doesn't get his way
He likes to sleep curled up in a ball
But he really should stop scratching the wall!

Whatever he sees, Bobby will eat
And he will watch the footballers on TV
He miaows at you when you eat
And he likes sitting on your feet
He climbs on me when I'm in bed
And purrs when I stroke his head
He's like a girl as he loves to keep clean
And he's the cutest cat I've ever seen!

Francesca Spolverino (10)

My Family

I thought of many people,
But
My favourite person is not one,
Not two,
But three favourite people.
In fact,
It is my family
They help me through the hardest moments,
They help me with the hardest subjects.
Let me tell you who they are,
There is my dad,
He is smart but funny,
My brother,
To me he is the cheeky one,
And not forgetting my mum,
She is there when I am down,
And always turns my frown upside down.

Lynne Davidson (11)

My Dog Choco

My glorious dog Choco is a Sprocker,
That's a cross between a Springer and a Cocker Spaniel.
A beautiful dog he is, chocolate-brown in colour,
His bright, adorable eyes light up my day in every way,
Especially when we play.

Our favourite game is soccer
But our game is short because Choco has very sharp teeth
And with a bang, the ball is busted.

He loves to go for a walk along a riverbank
Then go for a swim before we come home.

When out of the water he gets,
He shakes his coat which leaves me soaked.
But I don't mind because it's my dog Choco.

Jake Lafferty (9)

My Favourite Person

He is not just my brother,
He is my best friend.
No matter how much we fight,
I will always love him,
Even if I don't want to admit it.
We have that special bond,
That's only formed between siblings.
There are times he can make me cry,
And times he can make me mad.
But there are times he can make me laugh,
And times he can make me happy.
When he is away from home,
I miss him terribly.
I worry about him all the time,
Hoping that he's happy.
That's why my favourite person is
Callum.

Amy Langston (13)

My Favourite Person

I love my mum lots
She really is the best
And even when I'm not so good she still beats the rest.

I couldn't ask for more
She is out of this world
So even when we are apart
She is always in my heart.

My mum is always there for me
I try to help her out
Even if it means cleaning the rabbits out.

She does all the chores
And deserves a night out
My mum is the best without a single doubt.

Alex Gordon (10)

My Best Friend Deanne

My best friend Deanne,
She can turn a frown
Into a smile,
When you're feeling
Upset.

My best friend Deanne,
She understands
My little ways
And always shares her secrets
And dreams because she
Cares.

My best friend Deanne,
Worth more than gold.
She plays with me
And I play with her.
Best friends forever.

Eunice Koroma (7)

My Little Doggy Logan

My little doggy Logan
He likes to go on walks
If he was a human
He would talk and talk and talk.

My little doggy Logan
He likes to sing and dance
When he's not on a walk
He'll eat my sister's pants.

Logan is a troublemaker
He's a pain in the butt
He's even got a catchphrase
'Stop it, you hairy mutt!'

Becky Rose Knowles (10)

My Mom

My mom is so lovely,
she gives me cuddly hugs.
Oh my lovely mom.

She loves me so much,
she is always there for me.
Oh my lovely mom.

She comforts me when I'm hurt,
she will never forget me.
Oh my lovely mom.

She buys me lots of things,
she helps me with my homework.
Oh my lovely mom.

She always smiles at me,
she never lets me down.
Oh my lovely mom.

Matthew Buckby (8)

Untitled

My favourite person is my friend,
She always likes to play with me
And never leaves me out.

My friend is very nice and she is never nasty,
We used to go to the same school but I moved school
But we live on the same street so I still see her.

Me and my friend are always doing stuff together
Like having sleepovers, going to parties and all sorts of stuff.

Me and my friend are different in some ways,
But some ways the same,
But me and my friend are impossible to separate.

Me and my friend have known each other seven years
And will be friends forever and ever.

Katie Fairhurst (11)

My Mum!

My mum is the best,
Even when I am being a pest!
She never gets too stressy,
When my room is really messy.

She never fails to put a smile on my face,
and she is the only one who could teach me to tie my shoelace.
She helps me when I am upset,
And she is not the mother to fret.

My mum cheers me up when I am ill,
And keeps me warm when I am feeling a chill.
She turns grey skies to blue,
And helps when I have the flu.

She is lots of fun,
Her heart is so big it weighs a ton!
That's my mum!

Hannah Pomfret (11)

Mum You Are The Best!

I don't know what I'd do without you,
You've turned my skies from grey to blue!
You've helped me through this journey of life,
From ABC to using a knife!
You had me and you gave me care,
You taught me how to love and share!
Even when I'm in a bad mood,
You still give me drink and food!
I remember all the good times we've had.
Never have you made me sad!
You kiss me and cuddle me and put me to bed,
You taught me to read all the wonderful books I've read!
You feed me soup when I am ill, you work in Asda on the till!
I love you more than anything and will always love you more,
This whole wide world is an adventurous place and you have given me a tour!

Sameerah Shaikh (11)

Enzo

Someday he and I could
Run a country
Me, the Prime Minister
He my MP.

Someday he and I could
Play cricket for England
Me the batter
He the fielder.

Someday he and I could
Go to the moon
Me the explorer
Him the pilot.

Suddenly I remember
He is my dog
All he can be.

Ana Young (11)

My Hero!

My hero is a soldier,
Standing bold and tall,
My hero is an angel,
One that will never fall,
My hero is a star,
That is always shining bright
My hero is the moon
That shows you through the night,
My hero is a warrior
Always knowing what to do,
My hero is a saint
Who stays with you through and through,
Now you know what my hero is capable of,
But you don't know her name.
Well her name is my mummy, helping me through all the pain.

Alice Allen (14)

My Number 1 Mum!

My mum is sporty
but never naughty
she likes to swim
that's why she's slim.

She loves to run
especially in the sun
she's as fast as a leopard
chasing a shepherd

I like to swim and run
but only with my mum
it is ace
when we race
but my mum always wins
and has a smiley grin.

I couldn't have a better mum!

Lucy Turpin (11)

My Mother

You're my mum
And you're such fun
When we sit in a car
And drive so far
And then we come to met a river
I'm so cold I start to shiver
But there's no worries
Coz you're my mum
And you're such fun
Nothing can come in between us
Not a lorry, not a bus
Coz you're my mum
You're such fun
You're the best
Better than all the rest.

Sarmad Khan (8)

She

She is the one I can rely on
There when everyone else has gone
She puts a smile upon my face
But also sets my speedy pace
There to praise me when times are hard
And to play with me in our backyard
Always puts others before she
And bobs anyone's baby on her knee
She's the one to look up to,
I also like her hairdo!
Even though she's my mum
She's more like a sister or a best friend
To stand by me through thick and thin
And everyone knows she'd never sin
I love my mum very much
She's my favourite personality.

Charlotte Gosling (14)

My Grandma And Our Hobby, The Scrapbook

Grandma's scrapbook is a hoot
I love to spend time looking at pictures that are cute
There's one of me when I was two
With ice cream on my face
And one of Gran aged fifteen, with a freaky hairdo
She's saved her cards from years ago,
Sent on special occasions
And there are programmes from a show
She starred in many moons ago
She will look at them when she is old
And memories will make her smile.

Now my poem is in her book
Where future family will take a look.

Emmie Clark (11)

My Favourite People

My favourite people are my mum
And dad because they're great.
They let me do all sorts of things
And let me stay up late.
Daddy teaches me guitar
Mum lets me help cook.
We do desserts and others too
From her special book.
They help me with my homework
And run through it with me.
They let my friends come round and play
And sometimes stay for tea.
I know that I will surely love
My favourite people forever.
My favourite people, mum and dad
Are my favourite people *ever*!

Molly Ellis (9)

My Favourite Person

This person is young and tall
She likes to shop in the mall
She is a lot of fun
And doesn't weight a ton

She looks very pretty
And doesn't like kitties
In the family she is the clown
And cares a lot about the town

On holiday she likes to sunbathe
But doesn't like the caves
She cooks so very well
When you have a secret, she doesn't tell

Now it's time to say goodbye
'Cause now I'm going to eat my mum's pies.

Caitlin Penrice (11)

Aunty Ann

Aunty Ann is lots of fun.
She likes to go for walks in the sun.
Walks on the beach.
And sometimes she will eat a peach.
She doesn't like wine
But she likes to go outside when it's fine.
She doesn't like to be late.
But she is very good at fishing without bait.
She has never ridden a horse,
But she always finishes her main course.
She likes to go swimming
And is a manager for a living.
She likes to bake, so I'm told.
And she likes to visit the old.
She likes flowers.
And she likes climbing towers.

Glenn Doncaster (10)

My Daddy

My daddy is cool
My daddy rules
My dad is football mad
My daddy is sometimes bad
My daddy has short hair
He acts like a bear

But! I love my daddy

My daddy is very tall
My daddy likes to play pool
My daddy helps my mum
My daddy loves the sun
My daddy's in a band
He sometimes needs a stand

But! I love my daddy.

Victoria Deery (11)

My Mum, Kath

My mum is always there for me,
In everything I do.
She imagines things, and plays with me.
And makes me care in everything I do.
She helps me with my homework.
And polishes my shoes.
She looks after me, more than she should,
And lets me walk home from school.
She looks after me when I am hurt,
So I do the same to her,
Even when she is cross with me,
I know she loves me the same.
The last thing of all is we are unbreakable,
I know nobody can ever break us up,
Because love is the most important thing in life.
Love.

Arabella Dolores Petts (10)

Marc

(Mum's work colleague)

Image is everything,
To this cool dude.
He wears bling!
And he's a bit rude.
The best thing about Marc,
He's always up for a lark!
But he does try to steal my lunch,
So I just show him my fist and threaten to punch.
He has bad taste in music
Listening to it makes me feel sick!
He has a fancy car to park
He works with my mum
And he's a great deal of fun
And that's what I like about Marc!

Sally Pierse (10

This Person Is

This person is cool and fantastic,
This person recycles all our plastic.
This person likes to play football,
But he's not too busy when I call.
This person isn't such a toughie,
You will never find him scruffy.
This person really is the best,
Even when I'm a pest.
This person taught me my ABC,
This person really cares for me.
This person is over forty years old,
But this person is not going bald.
This person, if you haven't guessed,
Is someone I think is simply the best.
This is of course my *dad!*
PS: my mum is cool too!

Abbie Williams (10)

My Best Friend

I have this best friend,
She's always by my side,
Even when
I'm on a scary ride.
She's always so nice,
Just like a guide,
She makes me smile,
And I have never sighed.
We always play games,
We usually hide
In tic-tac-toe
We always tied!
When we're embarrassed
We keep our pride,
Since we are the greatest of friends.

Tyla Thomas (11)

My Mom

She is a working star,
Who has a job behind a bar,
She shops and cooks,
And reads a lot of books,
That's what you call a star!

She gets really tired at night,
So sometimes she fancies a pint,
She falls asleep,
And you won't hear a peep,
And that's what you call a star!

She hates screaming cats,
But cheered me on my SATs,
She loves her pets,
But hates going to the vets,
My favourite person is . . . *my mom!*

Tiegan Stanford (11)

Three favourite People

My mum makes my dinner
Makes me happy,
Makes me cakes,

I love my mum

My dad lets me play my computer
Makes me happy,
Gives me chocolate,

I love my dad

My sister helps me tidy my room,
Shares her chocolate with me,
Draws me pictures

I love my sister

Three favourite people I love.

Jack McElroy (10)

My Cat Arthur

His ears are like pricked pyramids.
His eyes are like two amber traffic lights
His smile is like a ray of sunshine coming through a stained glass window.
His face is full of kindness like a nurse as she treats a patient.

His fur is like a tiger's, but when he's sprawled out,
He can be mistaken for a thick ginger carpet.
His belly sags like a bag of sand would hang from a tree.
His tail is thick and bushy, similar to a fox's
His body's like a cuddly teddy bear,
Just being stuffed full of cotton wool.

Arthur is always there when I'm sad,
Happy, confused and angry.
That's why he's my best friend,
He's so full of love and I'm sure we'll be best friends,
Till death do us part.

Shannon Thwaite (11)

My Cuz

My favourite person, who could it be?
My favourite person, hmm let me see;
Ah! My baby cousin Michael!
Who is always happy as anyone can be,
His bib's always wet,
From his constant dribbling,
And his mouth never stops,
From all his giggling,
He's sooo cute when he sits in his doughnut,
Watching TV,
Laughing along with the songs and the characters,
Up on the screen.
My favourite person who can it be?
It's . . . ? my baby cousin Michael,
Don't you see!

Leah Scott (11)

My Sister

My sister is a star performer
She lives to entertain
She does her best
And gives her all
And it really pays off in the end!

She should be famous
The world's best singer!
She's a perfect role model
She is my inspiration
I'd love to be just like her when I'm older!

She has nerves of steel!
She looks after me when I'm ill
Always doing her best to protect me!
That's what I love about her!
She is always trying to keep me safe!

Hannah Giddens (11)

Forever Friends

Through tears and fights
Through smiles, I knew everything would be alright.
Through love and hate
Through trial and debate,
For you I would always have faith,
Being your sister as well as your best friend
I knew this friendship wouldn't end,
By your side I would always stand
And you'd stand by mine too
Because that's what best friends do,
So no matter what happens with us in life,
Through all the wrongs
And all the rights,
I'm here for you to be a best friend, that's true,
Because I love you and that's what best friends do.

Elizabeth Richards (11)

My Sister Fern

My sister Fern
Has blonde hair like sand glistening in the sun,
With brown highlights that dance in the wind,
And the best thing of all, she's my sister!

She sticks up for me through good and bad,
Even though I drive her mad,
She does gymnastics all the time,
With seven gold medals, a silver and a bronze in line,
And the best thing of all, she's my sister!

She helps me when I hurt myself,
Wipes my tears away,
She truly is my favourite person,
I couldn't ask for someone better,
And the best thing of all, she's my sister!

Lara Jobling(10)

My Favourite Person

My mum's my favourite person
She makes me currant buns
She keeps me clean
And makes me laugh
And gives me bubble baths.

My mum's my favourite person
I love her so much
She gives me lollipops
And care for me so much
And she looks after me when I'm ill
She helps me up when I fall over
And puts a plaster on my leg.

My favourite person is my mum
She is my best friend.

Amelia Robins (9)

Hannah Montana

Hannah is never shy
She has always got her head held high
She sings nice and loud
And she is proud.

Her friends never take pity
Because she is so pretty
She wears nice clothes
And wears fab shoes.

Hannah is never shy
She has always got her head held high
She sings nice and loud
And I bet she is proud.

Veerinder Kaur Gill (9)

My Dad

My dad is always there for me whenever I turn back
He always takes me here and there to buy a Lego pack
I really do love him, he is by far the best
Even though sometimes he really is a pest.

He likes to watch football live on TV
His favourite team is Aberdeen, especially when they score a goal or three
Gardening is his other passion
The flowers he plants always turn out smashing.

He is my friend and father too
Especially when I am feeling blue
He really is the best
Better than all the rest.

Finlay Cardno (10)

My Mum And Dad

M y parents are fun
Y oung

M um looks after me when I'm ill
U mbrellas are always taken out when raining
M obiles are used a lot by Mum

A lways willing to help someone
N ice all the time
D entists and doctors we hate going to

D ad's cool
A lways working hard
D edicated - and that's why I love them.

Melissa Ward (10)

My Favourite Person

My favourite person is a girl,
she can even sing in her own world.

She has her own songs and she is never wrong.
She begins with an L and ends with an A,
her name is Lady Gaga, and she is my favourite person today.

Her songs are the best,
so I hope no one will confess.
So many songs she has made,
even more than Rihanna and my best friend, Paige.

Her songs are different, and they're cool,
her first song took the same time as the long game, pool.

Tiffany-Jayne Bull (13)

Sisters At Heart

I've known you for a long time
But it seems that every time we meet,
The smile you always show me,
Is still brighter than the sun.
The time we spend together,
Can be seen through a window in our hearts,
For everyone to see, but for us to keep,
It is my most treasured possession.
And I'm sure through the years to come,
Both our lives will change,
But our relationship will stay strong,
Because we are sisters at heart.

Chloe Runkee (13)

Shanti The Rabbit

Shanti was our rabbit
She didn't have a single bad habit
When she passed away we all cried
The children didn't understand why she died
She was grey and furry
From far she looked blurry
We named her Shanti in Punjabi meaning peace
She sat beautifully on her hay and didn't make a single crease
We light candles and remember the good days
The way she jumped and ran different ways
She shall always be in our heart
And never will we be apart.

Mohammad Abdullah (13)

My Dog Ruby

My favourite person is my dog
Ruby is her name
She wags her tail and jumps about
She likes to play a game
Ruby is a boxer dog
And she is nearly three
I've had her since she was six weeks old
I know that she loves me
A week ago she had four pups
She has just become a mum
Three girls, one boy all very cute
But they all have stinky bums!

Nell McCall (6)

Me And My Dad

Me and my dad make a great team
Though it may not seem,
To the untrained eye we have a special bond.
I have always wondered if some fairy waved a magic wand,
To make this special bond.
My dad is clever; he does his engineering very well
About his day he always has something to tell
He always brings a boot load of paperwork
Though he sorts through it easily!
Me and my dad have a special bond
Like no other!
And so says my mother.

Alice Parkes (8)

She Means So Much To Me

My favourite person is my mom
Because she helps me get along.
Her positive attitude and wonderful tips
Will always help as soon as they leave her lips.
She's always right
And is my guiding light.
Even though she has five kids
Her love will always be so big.
I know she will be there to correct the things I've done wrong
And build me up until I'm strong.
I wrote this poem to make her see
How much I love her and to tell her that she means so much to me!

Emilie Riley (14)

My Hamster, Lucky

Lucky is my best friend
He sits there in the coolest trend,
His age doesn't matter or his size
But when he stares at me with those eyes,
He's always hungry, he always needs food
Even when he's tired he always looks good.
Squeak, squeak, squeak. Here we go again
Always on the wheel, drives me round the bend.
We need to clean the cage every week
If we don't, the room will reek.
It's Lucky's birthday in one day,
He's up and ready and out to play.

Kerri Lorraine (10)

Who To Choose?

It is very hard to choose,
But, what have I got to lose?
First of all there's my mother,
She's kinder than any other.
Then comes my dad,
He's really not that bad.
My sister comes next in line,
We get along all the time.
Oh no, this is too tough,
I give up, I've had enough.
I like them all the same
So I'm not going to say one name.

Merran Paxton (11)

Libby And Me

Libby's very funny and also very sweet,
We hate to be apart and always will be friends.
I've been to her house and played for hours and hours,
We meet up at school and then we choose our games.

If we can't choose our game then we do a dance until the end of break,
Now back in lessons we wish we were together.
In the holidays we see each other daily
We signed up for the talent show and did a rocking dance,
We also play snooker and sometimes we both win!

We play every day with smiles on our faces
And giggle when Buckaroo bucks!

Victoria Jenkins (8)

My Sister And I

We have always been together,
dancing through our teens together,
ate our greens together,
and with every year, you were always near.

Brought up as kids together,
counted our quids together,
borrowed pan lids together,
and when I needed you, you'd always come through.

Now were are still young together,
so let's enjoy the weather together.
my sister and I.

Alisha Allman (13)

Picnic

Hey, to everyone out there, guess what?
Picnic is my teddy bear.
He got named when we were in the countryside
and I got him when I was born, what a surprise.
He's got a little beige top and a nice red bow
he's got cool little eyes and a cute little nose.
Picnic's got a great big smile everyone knows.
I think about him every day and I hug him at night
and he takes his shades on holidays to keep the sun off his eyes.
He sleeps at nine at night and wakes up early in the morning.
He is my favourite little bear and also matches with my nice brown hair!

Isabelle Marie Rayworth (10)

Mouse

My golden retriever is weirdly named,
To sit and stay he has been trained,
He's far from small but rather nosy,
Sleeping in the light where he's cosy,
He likes his food and likes to run,
He's nearly the colour of the sun,
His tongue lolling out, his face full of wit,
He follows me everywhere and sits where I sit,
I love my dog and he's the key,
We belong together him and me,
I really hope we'll always be!

Bethany McTrustery (14)

My Angel In The Night

In the words of Shakespeare 'Shall I compare thee to a summer's day?'
I can't say I can compare him to anything more than a stroke of light in the darkness.
He is as bright as the sun, but as tough as nails, and you will never feel loneliness.
His blonde hair flies in the wind and his heart warms up the night and you will never feel coldness.
Even when you feel the word's crashing down he reminds you it is never the end.
That is why he is my best friend.

Emma Calvey (14)

My Favourite Person

My favourite person is my mum
She's the only one
She helps me through troubled times
And also makes me understand
I should not commit crimes
If my bedroom's not pristine
She can make a hell of a scene
So I would just like to thank you
Because no one else can do what you do
Thank you Mum
You're the one!

Jordan Brown (11)

My Nephew Ali

My favourite person has to be my nephew,
He's kind and caring,
Sweet and bubbly,
He knows how to make me cheerful when I'm sad,
He's always there watching over me,
He's my very own special and unique guardian angel,
My nephew is my inspiration and
Makes my living worthwhile,
If he wasn't here I would see no point in living,
He is my one and only
Favourite person.

Ibara Razaq (12)

Cameron

Cameron is a baby boy
He is active, funny and cute
He adores Thomas the Tank Engine
It drives me round the bend
He likes trying on other people's shoes
Sometimes he can be really annoying
I sometimes send him crazy
If I ever upset him, he says to me, 'Oh Anna!'
It sounds so cute.
His laugh is adorable
But I love him lots and he's my favourite person.

Rheanna Egleton (10)

My Favourite Person Is My Grandad

My grandad is, and will always be, my favourite person.
He took me everywhere, to the shops and to see the trains.
It didn't matter where anything was, he would take me anywhere.
When the sun was out, he would take me to the park.
He would push me on the swings, as high as we could go.
We would kick the ball around the garden, hopefully score a goal
and when it rained, we would sit and watch the television and read a book or two.
I loved spending time with my grandad, he always made me laugh.
I know he is still watching me. I can see him in the stars.
So this is for my grandad, my most favourite person ever.

Ashton Broxholme (6)

My Baby Cousin

My baby cousin is rather cute,
Banging on his toy drum after eating his fruit.
My baby cousin is wobbly when he walks,
And it makes hardly any sense when my cousin talks.
My baby cousin never cries, he laughs a lot instead,
He laughs and laughs, even when he bumps his head.
My baby cousin likes to bash, he'll bash anything he sees,
If he was on his own outside,
You'd find he'd be bashing on some trees.
But my baby cousin is the best, the best I'll ever know,
And I will love him more than ever, as I watch him grow!

Gemma Williams (11)

My Grandad

My favourite person was my grandad
Every time I think of him it makes me feel a little sad.
He was big and strong, he always made me feel safe.
He was a funny grandad, he taught me lots and made me laugh.
He helped my dad build my house.
My grandad lived right next door to me
So I could see him whenever I wanted.
I miss my grandad
His voice, his smell,
But at least I have the memories
In my big house that my funny, loving grandad built.

Olivia Jackson (10)

My Papa

My papa is a king and I am a princess
We explore the world together and save the queen
And battle with all of the hideous, fearsome monsters
Then we pick all of the roses
And eat all of the cheese on the moon
The Mars police chase us but we are so fast they don't catch us
If they did, we would be made to eat Brussels sprouts, yuck
But if they caught us, we would win.
Sergeant Mars would never make us eat Brussels sprouts!
At least that is what happens in my head
I love my papa.

Cara Marenghi (10)

Mum You're The Best - Forget About The Rest

She's nice
She's mad sometimes too
She's got good fashion
She likes animals too
Of course she likes music and
Dancing too, on Friday nights
Then there is one more thing
That you must know, oh yes
She likes Chinese food!

Iona Newman (10)

My Favourite Person

My mum is lovely
My mum works hard
My mum loves me like no one else.

My mum is lovely
My mum helps me
With problems that happen to me.

My mum is lovely
My mum is the best
My mum is my heart
I love you Mum.

Declan Whatmough (9)

Untitled

My mum is the best
Better than all the rest
She never lets me down
You will never see me with a frown.

She will always be there for me
Whenever I need to talk, she's always free
Whenever I start to cry
She comforts me and asks me why.

That's why my mum is the best
Better than all the rest!

Klaudia Robinson (10)

The King Of Pop Michael Jackson

The king of pop Michael Jackson
Gone too soon, I'll remember a flickering candle,
Under the moon, gone too soon.

His music and talent cannot be beaten
From 'Thriller' to 'Billie Jean'
A talent from afar can be seen

Although gone but not forgotten,
His music lives forever in our hearts.
Forever breaking the music charts.
RIP Michael Jackson, my friend.

Kyle Dunnel (11)

My Mum

My favourite person,
Is so sweet and kind!
When I think about her,
I can't get her out of my mind!

She does anything for me,
Anything at all!
Every time she's working.
She will always give me a call!

My mum, my mum, my mum is the best!
My mum, my mum, is never a pest!

Chloe McDonald (10)

My Mum

Me and my mum are two peas in a pod,
She's funny and I'm just odd,
She's now blonde and I'm brunette,
I always win if we make a bet,
She looks after me,
And lets me sit on her knee,
Whenever I am sad,
And it makes me so glad,
To be her daughter.
I love you mum

Sydney Horne (12)

My Mother

My mother would jump off cliffs for me;
My mother is always there to let me be.
My mother never lets me down;
Even choosing clothes in town.
Never-ending love for me, her precious girl;
She makes me feel like an outstanding pearl.
There's nobody whom I could love more;
I wonder if she could lock up her spare love in a drawer.
So, to conclude this poem of my mother,
I want to say, I would never wish for another.

Charlotte Marsh (11)

Anonymous

It is a she, who is special for me
We have lots of active fun, she is my chum
Sticking together, helping each other
We fight, talking to each other again is right
Getting up to adventures, my cousin sister.

Tanjima Akhtar (11)

My Sister

I have an older sister called Amirah
We have always shared a bedroom,
So, she always makes me happy, whenever I'm gloomy.
Together we go on adventures and sometimes to fairs,
We sit on thrilling rides as a pair.
We live in each other's hearts,
And sometimes we fall apart.
Whenever I look at her face,
I am assured that I am at the right place.
We always treat each other like special friends.

Zainab Sattar (13)

My Favourite Person

My favourite person in the whole wide world is my mummy
because I love to taste her yummy food.
I love my mummy because she gives me hugs which feel warm
and I feel like I'm at home.
I love my mummy so much because,
although I'm the only girl, she loves us all the same.
My mummy is like a box of yummy chocolates waiting to be eaten
She smells like red roses picked from Heaven.
My mummy means everything to me
and I would be nothing without her.

Aqsa Mahmud (11)

Michael Jackson

I like the 'Earth Song', but my hero is gone,
It's very sad, one of his best is 'Bad'
There's a song, it's a chiller, it's 'Thriller'
He turned from black to white
This is a very touching song, it's 'Black or White'.

Jamie-Lee Jaeger (10)

My Mum

My mum is my world
My mum is my happiness
My mum is my joy and also my pride
My mum is my tears
My mum is my eyes
My mum is my laughter and is also my heart
My mum is my music
My mum is my toys
My mum is my glasses and is also my angel
My mum is my mum.

Jack Stiles (11)

All About Ashley Tisdale

When I look at her performing in films and concerts
I think, wow she is so lucky
I have always wanted to be an actress
But sometimes I don't think I will have a chance to be one
Maybe even meet her as a reward, in little groups, we will never know
I have first seen her in 'HSM' and 'Suite Life of Zack and Cody'
And other films, she must have been in loads
But here I am writing this hoping that I might stand out in this competition!

April Lukanu (11)

My Mummy

Mummy is great because she bakes cakes with me
She goes to work to buy me lots of toys
And get pennies for us to take on holiday to Turkey.
I love my mummy because she is pretty and funny
And she is the best mummy in the world.

Lauryn Dickinson (7)

Me And Mary

Me and Mary go to the park
Me and Mary fish in the dark
Me and Mary make loud farts
Me and Mary like apple tarts
Me and Mary collect lots of bark
Me and Mary like the dark
Me and Mary love to swim
Me and Mary go to the gym
Me and Mary together we'll be
Me and Mary, Mary and me.

Samantha Hardman (10)

My Mom

I love my mom, she is great
She really is my number one mate.
She cooks and cleans and make my tea
She really does look after me.
She makes me happy when I'm sad
She really makes me feel so glad.
She takes me with her wherever she goes
I never ever get under her toes.
So I'm sending my mom lots of hugs and kisses
And lots and lots of sweet wishes.

Danielle Davies (9)

Fruit

Oranges and lemons they're so juicy and nice,
I could eat them with a pot of rice,
Bananas and grapes are good for the apes,
Strawberries and pineapple are so great,
I could eat them with my mate.

Emma Ferguson (11)

My Mum

My mum is number one,
Always lets us have lots of fun,
All day we play in the sun,
She is the best, far better than all the rest.
If I am ever down
I can never frown,
Because she is always there,
We make such a great pair,
I know she will always care,
That's my mum, my best chum.

Jordan Burnett (8)

My Favourite Person

This person looks after me when I'm down,
She's always clowning around.
To cheer me up she's making funny faces,
Even when I'm tying my shoelaces.
I always laugh and giggle or
Roll around and wriggle.
If I'm not having fun,
She'll do a dance whilst eating a bun.
This is my favourite person.
This is my mum.

Hazera Begum (9)

My Best Friend

People near, people far, look at this, it's a shining star.
It shines with courage, humour and trust.
It shines with kindness, friendship and love.
So everyone look at the light
The star you seek is *Sophie White*.

Holly O'Connor (10)

The Best Dad

My favourite person is my dad
I keep him company when he is sad.
When I sit on his knee,
He makes me laugh with glee.
He's funny then cool!
Suddenly he jumps directly into my pool.
He loves watching sports.
But he's only been on a few squash courts.
But all I want is my favourite person.
My dad.

Abigail Munro (9)

My Dog

My dog, Star, has a black wet nose
Two big brown eyes
And a spotty freckled nose
Two floppy ears
A long bushy tail
Four fast legs
And four hand shaking paws
A giddy personality
And a whopping great big smile
That is my dog, my dog, Star

Georgia Thornton (8)

My Best Friend

My best friend keeps our friendship together as powerful as glue,
This is how I know, she is . . .
Adventurous, always hungry, a handful, always right, artistic, closest person ever, creative, chocolate taker, song writer, scared - *never*, sports star, surprising, sharer, sleepyhead, tomboy, thoughtful.

Asha Wilkinson (10)

My Favourite Person

My favourite person is the one who cares for me,
The one who gives me support,
The one who gives me so much love in my life,
And who also protects me from people who try to harm me.
She is the one who comforts me when I'm sad,
She is the one who brings light to me when I'm left in the darkness
When the heat from the sun becomes unbearable,
She will come to me as my shade,
She is truly amazing and extraordinary,
And that woman is my mum.

Mohammad Ibara Ali Razaq (12)

My Favourite Person

My mum helped me in many ways,
But when I try to count, there are uncountable days.
Whenever I see her glowing face,
It reminds me that in my heart, she has a very special place.
She raised me with love,
And flies with me in life, like a dove.
She has her own unique trends,
And I know she will always be my special friend.
She fills and completes my life with her smiles,
These memories go on for miles and miles.

Amirah Sattar (17)

Lucky

My favourite person is strong and brave you see
I love them because they're always there for me.
My favourite person is Mum, you might hear that a lot
But my mum is the best, better than the rest
She is my one and only favourite person.

Nicole Thorneycroft (13)

My Nanna

I know someone who is special to me,
Someone who I am always happy to see.
She makes me toast,
Hot chocolate too.
She makes me laugh,
From here to the moon.
I love her and
She loves me,
When I am with my nanna
To my heart, she holds the key.

Declan Parker (11)

Baby Daniel

Baby Daniel, his shiny blue eyes, and hair as soft and blonde as a lion.
Always I will love him, my brother and best friend.
Beautiful is his smile, to match his chubby cheeks.
You will always be gorgeous, baby Daniel, both young and old.
Daniel, I know you care about the world
And you love it when I sing songs to you.
Never do you make me sad,
In fact, you always make me glad.
Even when I'm feeling down
Love and laughter's all around.

Courtney Legan (11)

My Mum

My mum is my best friend and secrets we do share
A shoulder to cry upon when I am sad and warm hands
To hug me and make me feel glad
A big warm heart that really does care and we will always be
Together till the end because you are truly my best friend.

Shannon Miller (10)

All About My Dad

My dad, Paul Plumber always says his job's a bummer.
When I am at school, I am really sad, but when I get home,
I see my dad.
Him smoking day by day, I think his life might pass away.
When I've got the coughs,
When I've got the sniffles,
My dad always cheers me up with lots of tickles.
He loves football, he loves life, that is why he is most important
in my life.
Happy or sad, I always know, I've got my dad.

Jordyn Rosser (11)

My Mum

My favourite person is my mum
She helps me complete my sums
She's the greatest person I've had
She's always with me when I'm sad
She's my mum that's why I'm glad
My mum's the one I've always had
She stayed awake when I was ill
And always remembered to give me my pills
She's the one who fed me on time.
My mum.

Lubabah Khan (11)

My Favourite Person

My mum is my favourite person
She is the person that I love from everyone in the world
She's the best and she beats the rest
Every minute of the day
I think she is great, OK.

Melissa Rodda (10)

My Brother

Badminton is what he likes to play,
So when will he choose to start today?
Called Ben, he is yet towering above me.
With two years apart still taller he may be,
But so very clever is he.
Ben's birthday's on the twenty-ninth of August.
Ben is like a star in the sky that will be forever.
He and me get along together.
Ben, the boisterous, brilliant and the best bro ever!

Emma Caro (9)

My Mum

My mum is so fair
And she is so caring
Whenever there's trouble
She helps me with things
And she makes me feel as if I am a king
When I'm hungry
So cooks me food
I think the food's crumbly
And when I taste the food it is so good.

Siril Sunny (10)

My Dog Sid

He's my best friend on Earth,
He always digs up our turf,
Always there for me,
Especially when I have my tea,
I love it when he wags his tail,
And when he eats the mail,
My dog, Sid.

Daniela Windram (11)

Roxy And I

Roxy and I, my cute dog, play together like we should.
We run together,
Shout together,
Eat together,
Eleep together,
Leap together,
Dance together,
and prance together.
We do everything together!

Sophie Newton (8)

Fun!

I have a friend, the best friend in the world.
We share things together and we share the whole wide world.
We are just like sisters, we have the hip hop
We will dance all night and boogie a lot.
We play around and have lots of fun.
We go on adventures although we're young.
We've had the sleepovers, we've had the nights.
We've had the times, we've had a fight.
But we always make up and have a good night.

Heather Robertson (10)

My Mum

My mum is always there for me every step of the way,
My mum is always caring no matter what happens.
My mum is the best mum
She's such a great person,
You'd be mad not to see her,
My mum is the best.
She makes the best things and that's why she's the best mum.

Jason Poom (9)

My Big Brother

My favourite person is my big brother,
He supports me through thick and thin,
And I love him.
He's funny and joyful,
Typical but lovable,
Stinky but huggable.
He's my brother, he's special in his own way,
He's my funny, joyful, typical, lovable, stinky and huggable, brother
I love him being my brother.

Elly Jackson (11)

My Family

I love my family because they do everything for me.
They have got me a kitten, that's how much they love me
And all my family likes football.
My favourite person is my mummy
Because she buys me lots and lots of stuff.
She has taken me to Liverpool, it was fun
And she took me to the Beatles shop
And she has done my room up
And taken me on holiday.

Ella Hull (8)

My Dad

My dad is great and he is a clown
He buys me lots and lots of tapes from the market
He is still like a clown
Because he is very funny.
He lets me watch TV
And I love him lots and lots
Because he is my dad.

Luke Richardson (6)

Mum

I love my mum, she is fun
Happy and jolly, that's why I love my mum

  M is for marvellous,
  U is for understanding and
  M is for making sure I am always safe

She is pretty and she never lets me down,
She always keeps a brave face through all troubled times.
That's why I love my mum.

Katherine Gill (11)

My Favourite Person!

  H appy and joyful
  A ngelic and cute
  N oisy and bouncy
  N utty to boot
  A dorable and pretty
  H annah is her name!

She is my niece and I love her
In every single way!

Charlotte Wade (11)

My Dog Penny!

She's playful and cute and very, very fast
If she was in a race she wouldn't come last.
She's black and brown and a little bit white
She nibbles my elbow when we play fight.
She's very well trained, she can lie down and sit
She'll give you her paw, if you ask her for it.
When she walks fast she does a little trot
This is my dog Penny, and I love her a lot!

Natasha Chappell (11)

I Have A Friend Inside My Head!

I have a friend inside my head
From dawn till dusk till I go to bed.
She whispers all the time to me,
Amber is what a true friend should be.

She never glares or scowls or smirks
She knows how everything inside me works.
Amber is there – like it or not,
I don't mind, I like her a lot.

Frankie Tulley (11)

My Favourite Person

Well that's a hard question to answer
Could it be my mum or dad, brother or grandparents
My uncle or auntie, my cousins or even my pets?

As I wonder,
As I think even harder,
I realise everyone who cares for or loves me,
And I care for and love,
They are all my favourite people!

Chloe Anne Hunter (11)

My Mum

My mum helps me with things I cannot do,
my mum helps me with my homework,
my mum takes me to great places,
my mum cares for me when I have got flu.

My mum gives the best hugs in the world,
my mum cares for others,
my mum is really funny,
my mum makes us do as we are told.

Emily Allen (11)

Untitled

J oe makes me happy, Joe makes me crazy and I have a lot of fun
O h my God, seeing him in November, hope I meet him he'll sign my shoe
E very day thinking of him.

J oe's the best, he never gives up
O pposite me singing to me, blow me a kiss and you will see.
N o singer can beat him, he sings so great, voice so good.
A picture of me and him that would be a dream come true.
S houting in concerts, going mad, let's go Joe, jump into the crowd.

Nikaela Cruikshank (11)

My Loving Father

My dad's a loving father,
He's a wonderful man
He's the joker of the pack,
And my number one fan.

My dad has always loved me,
Each morning to night,
I've always loved him back,
For he is my bright light.

Daniel Morton (11)

My Favourite Person

My favourite person is my mum
She looks after me and is lots of fun.
And though she sometimes gets mad
And sometimes she's very sad
She still goes to work to earn money
And takes me places when it's sunny.
One last thing about my mum
She gives me money to buy bubblegum.

Eilidh-Jane Murphy (10)

I Can't Describe My Mum

I can't describe my mum.
Is it magic? Is it great?
I can't describe my mum.
Why is it, she's never late?
I can't describe my mum,
With her I can't compare.
I can't describe my mum,
Oh wait, she'll always care!

Dylan Foster (10)

Untitled

It's hard to find the words to say,
How much Mum means to me.
She's caring and helpful,
And rather delightful.
She's hard-working all the time,
And helps me play the chime.
It's hard to find the words to say,
How much Mum means to me!

Falak Khan (7)

My Favourites

I have a family unlike any other,
A mum, a dad, one sister and four brothers.
I love them all dearly with all of my heart,
Each and every one of them, I'd give full marks.
They're all so special in every way,
They can't fly nor save the day.
They're funny and helpful, they love to rest
So why have one favourite when they're all the best?

Lauren Richardson (12)

My Cat Fluffy

My cat Fluffy has a very long, black tail,
She shimmers in the light,
Because of her soft, shiny, silky black fur.
She pats you with her gentle soft paws.
She looks at you lovingly with her big green eyes.
Using her sharp, playful teeth, to play with her toy rabbit.
She miaows with delight, whenever she sees me.
That's why I will always love my little black cat, Fluffy.

Shannon Hill (10)

My Parents

I don't have one favourite person, you see,
And my brothers all agree with me.
I think they're the best parents ever found,
I think they're the greatest people around.
They're the best people I've ever known
With them around we're never alone.
Our mum and dad always help us all
And pick us up each time we fall.

Elizabeth Lovejoy (12)

Untitled

My friend is like a flower,
A rose to be exact or a gate that has never been unlatched.
My friend is like an owl,
So beautiful and wise.
My friend is like a heart,
That stays by my side.
My friend will stay with me till the end.
What would I do in this world if I didn't have a friend?

Tianna Costelow (11)

My Favourite Person

My favourite person is my sister
Her name is Sophie McCulloch.
She is the best sister ever
And we sometimes play together.
We play outside
But when it is raining, we play inside.
I love my sister,
She is the best.

Neal McCulloch (9)

Chips The Monkey

Chips, a rockin' build-a-bear monkey.
Fun, cool and stylish.
Like a bunch of flowers, pretty and fresh
Like a teddy bear, cute and cuddly.
I feel good when I'm with him.
Like your heart, you can't live without it
Chips, it reminds us how special
Some things make us feel.

Hannah Chambers (11)

The Ultimate, Cool Mum Is A Favourite

There's an ultimate, cool mum who lives down the crooked street
She is really great, she deserves a massive, fab treat
She really does care
She's never a spare
I love her so much, she's the best
Her attitude's cool, it's better than the rest.
No one wants her leaving or ever to go
So that's why the ultimate, cool mum is a favourite.

Sabia Shafiq (10)

My Favourite Person

My favourite person is Morgan. She is my best friend.
We'll be together until the very end.
She is very nice
And is terrified of mice.
She is nine years old the exact same as me
And we met in Primary 3.
She likes school and thinks it's cool,
She loves art and her pink go-kart.

Yasmin Martin (9)

My Mum

She is so pretty just like a rose,
And if you smell her with your nose,
She smells so sweet, even good enough to eat,
But only ever as a treat.
She is so kind,
Imagine that in your mind,
It makes me feel that something like that couldn't be mine,
As I love her all the time.

Dillon Marsden (11)

Dad
(My favourite person)

My Dad . . . well what can I say!
He goes to fix lasers every day,
He watches footie, but fishing's his thing.
He casts right out, watch the rod fling!
He thinks he's the best . . .
Better than me . . . but when it comes to fishing
I'm the daddy!

Sam Knapman (11)

My Favourite Popstar

I dreamt I was Lily Allen,
That star I liked so much.
She looked good at Wembley,
The fans all wanted to touch.
She earned a lot of money, for singing on the stage.
She spent it all on toffees, her dad was in a rage.
She got so fat from eating sweets, Miss Piggy she became.
No one liked her anymore, Lily Allen lost her fame.

Jessica Milner (9)

My Friends

I have one friend, she is cheerful,
She likes to befriend, but is never fearful.
I have one friend, she is kind,
She will defend, but never minds.
I have one friend, she is chatty,
She will comprehend, but she's never too batty.
I have three friends, they are brilliant,
We make amends and we're resilient.

Phoebe Corser (15)

My Friend Lara

Lara is special,
She is my friend,
Lara makes me smile,
Our friendship is strong and will not end,
To me, Lara is the sun on a summer's day,
Because the sun plays with the trees,
And me and Lara together,
We are always ready to play all day long!

Catarina Alves (8)

My Limited Edition Mum

My limited edition mum,
Is so special and is never glum!
She's got blonde short hair,
But is allergic to sweet pears.
My mum would always put us first no matter what.
She loves all of us, me and my three brothers.
She's not like other mothers
Like I said, she's a *limited edition mum!*

Rhiannon Burrows (12)

My Brother

He was always there for me
My face for him to see
He always helped me when I was in need
And took care of me as if I was his seed
Though we fight all day long
Our hearts will always stick to each other mighty and strong
When we play together it is like picking beautiful shells
He is my favourite person and will always be in my heart and soul.

Abdul Baasit Mahmood (11)

Spring Is Something Special

She runs through the wind as fast as it blows
So that she is there when the sky turns black
She frightens the darkness and sadness away
She lights up the world when the sun disappears
She smooths out my heart when the edges are rough
She takes away pain and replaces it with peace
She laughs when I laugh, she'll die when I die
Because as long as I'm living, she'll live in my heart.

Eleanor Gabriel (10)

My Best Friend

Rowan is like a sweet little flower growing in my garden.
She is as peaceful as a quiet countryside, relaxing and calm.
Rowan is like an artist concentrating on her work.
She is as clever as a professor working in her lab.
Rowan is like a snowflake falling on my head.
She is as calm as a bird relaxing on a tree.
Rowan is as cheeky as a cheeky monkey playing games with me.
She is as pretty as a butterfly on my hand.

Lauren Siely (9)

Untitled

I don't really have a favourite person
But this is someone who is there for me
And looks after me as a mom should
Like cooking for me
Playing football with me
And feeding me healthily
And checking I'm OK and
Teaching me stuff to do with school work.

Adam Wilkinson (11)

My Mum's A Supermum

My mum is a supermum
She's really good to me
She's always very sensible
She's very kind and nice
She does so many different jobs
And all of them for free
She's a supermum and no one else
Could love her like I do!

Aimee Ford (11

My Favourite Person

For my poem, I've chosen my mum
Because if I need her she will come
I love seeing her heart-warming smile
Even when I'm naughty and in denial
She is always there for me.
And makes the most delicious tea
That is why I chose my mum
Because she is a really good chum.

Alexander Jessiman (11)

My Mum

My favourite person is my mum.
She wakes me up in the morning and packs my lunch.
She takes me to school.
School is a lot of fun.
She picks me up after school.
We talk as we go home.
My mum is a one and only.
And that is what I love about my mum.

David Triano (10)

My Favourite Person

My favourite teacher
Was a teaching creature
Though I found it tough
And I've had enough
But I never gave up
Like a little pup
In the end
I pretended I was French.

Claudia Law (10)

William

The moon's shining in the sky
and I wonder if you're watching it too?
Sound asleep and all I dream of
is waking up to see you
I still count the seconds we are apart;
because without you I am not myself.
I love you and know my heart is yours to make or to break,
to love or hate for even death cannot part us.

Gemma Wells (12)

My Favourite Person

My very favourite person was very hard to choose.
I thought about it for a while, but found someone who couldn't lose.
My very favourite person is someone who's always there,
Who's always filling me right up with their tender loving care.
She helps me with my homework if ever I get stuck,
And washes my clothes continuously as they always come back in muck.
Sometimes we go shopping and sometimes we stay in,
But whenever, wherever we are together this title my great mum wins.

Jodi Morgan (11)

The Queen

My favourite person is the Queen
She's always too busy to be seen.
She wears a crown and a very long cloak,
And waves her hands to friendly folk.
She has two corgis that roam the grounds,
Her head is even printed on five pounds.
She is my favourite person, I do know,
Because she makes my money box grow.

Thomas Oliver (10)

My Loving Mum

Mums are very special
Because they're always there
They take the time to listen
When worries cloud your days
And how I am forever grateful
In many different ways
I'm never able to find the words
To tell my mum how much I care.

Kimberley Breingan (11)

My Mum

My mum is called Marie.
My mum is married to Richard.
My mum has a dog and two cats.
My mum makes bread and soup really well.
My mum's favourite colour is red.
My mum is the best mum ever!
I love my mum!

Shannon Turney (10)

Mystery

Nice as a flower
Tall as a tower
Loves to play cricket
Sweats like rain
Hide-and-seek is his game
He is a friend and an enemy
He's a mystery. . . ?

Tajalla Rasool (12)

My Favourite Person

My favourite person is a great footballer
He's scored four against my brother's favourite team,
He's number 23
He plays for my favourite team,
His shots are lethal,
And he's got lightning pace and skill,
And he's a Russian and Arsenal star.

Brandon Parkin (10)

My Mum And Dad

My mum and dad are the best thing that happened to me,
from the day I was born to the day I will die
my mum and dad are always there for me.
They always make me smile when I see them.
They're always looking out for me.
That's why I could not pick between one of them.
My favourite people are my mum and dad.

Amy Louise Crain (11)

My Dad

He's my favourite person and I never say,
He gets up really early and crams so much in one day,
He drives me round in the car and gives me pocket money,
And when we are at parties, he dances really funny,
He's the one that hugs me close and stops me feeling sad,
Yes, that's right, you guessed it,
Because it is my dad.

Megan Jarvis (10)

I Love My Dad

My favourite person is my dad.
He calms me down when I am mad.
That is why I love my dad.
He is the funniest dad that kids have ever had.
He picks me up when I am sad.
I am very, very glad I have my dad.
I couldn't wish for a better dad.

Jamie Lee Hopps (10)

Best Friend

You are my only friend
always there with time to spend
but when you're gone I feel really sad
and when you're back it makes me glad
you are always there by my side
get in the car, let's take a ride
you are my only friend.

Arooj Khan (10)

My Favourite Person

My favourite person is my mummy.
She's the best mum you could ever have.
My mum does everything for me.
She has black hair and green eyes
And gives hugs and kisses to me
And is as nice as can be,
That's why she's my favourite.

Matthew Whelan (6)

A Thanks To Dad

My dad has made my holiday fun
By going places in the summer sun.
I enjoyed the beach, the pool, the walks,
Wherever we went,
We always talked.
But most of all, I'd like to say,
Thank you Dad, for a super summer holiday.

Katelyn Grant (11)

Grandma

G reat and amazing I know she loves me,
R adiant and glowing, she is full of glee.
A ll together, she is the best,
N o doubt she will beat the rest.
D elightfulness I give to her,
M y grandma's not a cat but if she was she would purr.
A nd that is my grandma!

Kayleigh Wickenden (10)

A Friend Is . . .

A friend is violet flowers growing in the spring.
A friend is a happy summer's day where everyone is happy.
A friend is a love heart who knows you are excited.
A friend is a swimming pool that you can splash in.
A friend is a chocolate cake making you hungry.
That friend is Jemma.

Beth Cushnie (9)

My favourite Person

My favourite person is my friend Georgia.
We do things together, run, jump, skip and climb
But never fall out,
We are alike.
The everlasting gobstopper
We will be friends forever and ever, ever and ever . . .

Abbie Kiernan (8)

My Friend Jack

My friend Jack
is like a flapjack
He reminds me of a giraffe
from his head and his neck
and he's nearly as tall
as a baby giraffe.

Arron Finnis (9)

Dream

When I grew up I grew up to be just like my mum.
Happy, bubbly, outgoing and my number one favourite, loving.
I had a great job like my mum,
I brought up my children well,
But then I heard a door slam
Then noticed it was all a dream.

Tahlia Walker (11)

An Ode To Mum

A snowy winter's night when the glimmering moon shines upon
the silver frozen lake.
Snow falling onto the frosted trees like icing sugar onto a cake.
Icicles still in their frosty sleep.
A blanket of snow and frosted rings,
You, Mum, remind me of all these wonderful things.

Sam Patrick (10)

Young Writers Information

We hope you have enjoyed reading this book - and that you will continue to enjoy it in the coming years.

If you like reading and writing poetry drop us a line, or give us a call, and we'll send you a free information pack.

Alternatively if you would like to order further copies of this book or any of our other titles, then please give us a call or log onto our website at www.youngwriters.co.uk

Young Writers Information
Remus House
Coltsfoot Drive
Peterborough
PE2 9JX
(01733) 890066